ALL ABOUT ENGLISH

⁕ Elizabeth and John Seely ⁕

Oxford University Press 1990

Contents

Part B: Reading   65

Part C: Writing   85

Part A: Knowledge about language

1: What language is

Getting the message across

Most species of animals have ways of sending messages to each other.

Bees Bees send out scout bees to find flowers with pollen. The scout bees can tell the other bees where to go for pollen *and* how far away the flowers are. They do this by performing a dance inside the hive.

1. If the flowers are near they do the round dance.

2. If they are further away they do a figure-of-eight dance. The further away the flowers are, the fewer times they do the dance.

3, 4, 5. They show the direction of the flowers by the angle at which they do the dance.

Human beings Human beings can also communicate without using words.

People and language

Signs and gestures have their uses, but most of the time we use words to get our message across.

Language is one of the most important things that separates human beings from other animals. No one really knows how language started, although many people have very interesting theories about it.

Whatever the truth of these theories, today language is worldwide, essential to our lives, and very varied indeed. These are some of the ways you might hear people greeting each other in Britain.

World languages   It is difficult to know exactly how many separate languages there are in the world. Most experts agree that the number is probably between 4000 and 4500. Some languages, like English, are spoken all over the world, by millions of people. Others, like some of the languages of Southern Africa, are spoken by fewer than 1000 people.

What's language for?

To express our feelings

We use words when we are very happy, or sad, or hurt, or pleased, to tell other people, and ourselves, how we feel.

To help us get on with other people

When we meet people and talk to them about the weather, or their pet cat, what we are really doing is saying, 'Oh hullo, yes, I know you, we get on all right together, don't we?'

To communicate ideas and information to other people

This is what most people think language is for. It is certainly a very important way in which we use language. (Also, of course, we use language to gain information from other people by asking questions.)

For fun

People also use words to give themselves, and other people, pleasure. They enjoy the sounds of words and the patterns they can make; they like to invent their own worlds using words. This is how poets and other creative writers use language.

To record information for the future

Writing can also be used when we want to make sure that important information is not forgotten. Ever since human beings have been able to write, they have used language to record information.

To help us work things out

When we are trying to do something complicated, it helps to think it out in words. You may even say the words out loud as you think. This is not a sign of madness, as people sometimes say; everybody does it from time to time.

Talking it through

Sometimes a good way to work things out is to talk them through with other people. You will find that your words and ideas set off other people's, and then what they say makes you think of something new.

Thinking and learning

A very important use of language starts as soon as we are born. Babies and young children learn their language – usually from their parents and those around them. They learn that things have names. This helps them to understand how different things are grouped together. Very early on, children also learn *about* language. For example, they learn that it can be used to get things done.

2: Speaking and listening

What is involved

Have you ever thought how much we depend on speaking and listening? If you are in any doubt about this, do a little experiment. Try to get through a whole day without talking, without saying a single word. (It is a lot more difficult to get through a whole day without listening, but you could get some idea of what it is like by watching television without the sound on.) It is very difficult, as speaking and listening are so *natural* to us. Yet when we examine exactly what they involve, we begin to see just how complicated they actually are.

Speech sounds   There are over forty different sounds in English words. They are made using the lungs, the throat, the mouth, the tongue, even the nose.

Stress and intonation   The two words 'Look out' can be said in many different ways. You can probably imagine how the person in the picture is saying them!

Using your eyes   When we speak we use gestures, movements of the body, to help us communicate. When we listen we observe the behaviour of the speaker, and this helps us to understand what is being said. The two children in the canoe can *see* that the person on the bank is very worried about something.

The situation   There are tens of thousands of words in English. The number of sentences you can make with them is uncountable. If we just had to rely on hearing the words, we might have to think quite a long time before we could understand what they meant. The children may not be able to hear clearly what is shouted at them, but can guess what it is from the situation.

Speech sounds

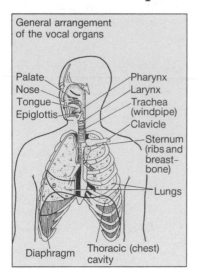

General arrangement of the vocal organs

Palate
Nose
Tongue
Epiglottis
Pharynx
Larynx
Trachea (windpipe)
Clavicle
Sternum (ribs and breast-bone)
Lungs
Diaphragm
Thoracic (chest) cavity

Sound is produced by making air vibrate. When we speak we use air which is pushed up out of our lungs and up the windpipe. This air is then vibrated by different parts of the throat and mouth. We can make different musical notes by using the vocal cords in our throats. These notes are used in speech. We use our mouths to shape the vowels and consonants that make up words.

Experiment

Stand in front of a mirror so that you can see clearly the movements of your mouth, lips, tongue, and teeth. Say the separate sounds of the words 'Look out', one at a time. Observe the movements you make to say the sounds. Now say the words at normal speed and be aware of how your mouth moves:

a. as you can see it in the mirror, and
b. as you can feel it moving inside.

That shows you what is involved in saying two short words. In normal speech you may speak at up to 200 words a minute!

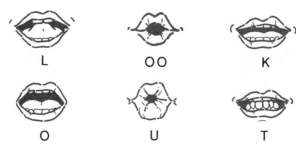

L   OO   K

O   U   T

Vowels   Vowels are sounds which are made with the mouth open all the time.

Experiment

Look in a mirror again, and try saying the middle sound in each of the words in the list. How does your mouth move as you go through the list? Look at the pictures: which sound do you think each one illustrates?

beat   bit   bet   bat   but
heart   hot   sort   put   fool

Consonants   When we say consonants, we block off the passage of air from the lungs. Sometimes we block it off for the amount of time it takes to say the consonant.

Experiment

Look in the mirror. Watch how you say each of these sounds:

m as in *mat*   **n** as in *neat*
ng as in *sing*

Each time you have blocked off the air from your lungs completely. How did you do this for each sound?

With most consonants, the air is partly blocked and partly allowed through. Sometimes this is quite slow. Watch what happens when you say:

f and **sh** as in *fish*

Sometimes it is quicker, more like a minor explosion. Observe how you say:

p and **t** as in *pat*

Stress and intonation

Intonation

Sentences have tunes. Often the same sentence can be said with two different tunes: changing the tune actually changes the meaning. The sentence, 'I'm walking round to see Marion.' has to be said with a falling tune at the end. This makes it clear that it is a statement.

The mother makes her voice go up at the end of the sentence. This makes it clear that she is asking a question. Not all questions use this rising tone. When we ask questions that start with question words, then we usually use a falling tone at the end of the sentence:

Where's my anorak?
Who's taken it?

Intonation is not just a question of whether your voice rises or falls at the end of the sentence. The whole sentence has a tune, and your voice can go up and down several times in the course of one sentence.

It isn't worth going on the bus.

No. I meant: You're walking round to see **Marion**?

Why not? She is my best friend.

Experiment

Try saying this sentence. Observe when and how your voice goes up and down as you say it.

Would you like a cup of tea, a Coke, an ice-cream, or nothing at all?

Stress

We say some parts of a sentence louder than others. This helps us to make clear exactly what we mean.

If you think about these two pictures, it is clear that the Mother must have said:

'You're WALKing round to see Marion?'

So her daughter thinks she is surprised that she is not cycling, or riding on the bus. In fact, what the mother meant to say was:

'You're walking round to see MARion?'

Stress means saying a word or part of a word with more force. Correct use of stress in sentences is an important part of clear communication.

17

3: The written word

Different writing systems

Different languages use different systems for writing down the words and sentences of speech.

Pictograms

The earliest writing systems were based on pictures. If you wanted to *record* something you drew a picture of it. A series of pictures could represent a simple message.

The problem with pictures is that they can have several different meanings. In modern times we use pictures as symbols, but we have to make sure that people understand what they mean.

Ideograms

Another problem with pictures is that some words and ideas are impossible to draw. So pictures gradually changed and gave way to symbols and signs. These could be used to stand for words that were difficult or impossible to draw as ordinary pictures. At the same time, writing became less like drawing and more like a system of signs that could be used more quickly.

Whole word languages

There are a number of languages today that use written symbols to represent whole words. One of these is Chinese.

大	(da) big
人	(ren) person
大 人	(daren) adult/grown-up

Syllable languages

Other languages use signs which represent parts of a word – syllables. (For example, there are two syllables in other: OTH-ER.) Modern Japanese uses a syllable system.

Hiragana syllabary

さようなら   (sayōnara) goodbye

Katakana syllabary

スカート   (sukāto) skirt

Alphabet languages

In other languages, symbols are used to represent the individual sounds that make up words. The advantage of this is that you have to learn far fewer symbols. English school children have to learn 26 symbols: the letters of the alphabet. Japanese school children have to learn 881 symbols during their first six years at school!

Russian alphabet

АБВГДЕЖЗИЙКЛМНОПР
СТУФХЦЧШЩЪЫЬЭЮЯ

Arabic alphabet

ص ض ط ظ ع غ ف ق ك ل م ن ٥ و ي
ا ب ت ث خ ح ج ث ت خ د ذ ر ز س ش

Deranagari alphabet
(The script for the Hindu language)

अ आ इ ई उ ऊ ऋ ए ऐ ओ औ क ख ग घ ङ
च छ ज झ ञ ट ठ ड ढ ण त थ द ध न
प फ ब भ म य र ल व श ष स ह

19

Writing English

English, like many languages, uses a writing system based on letters. Groups of letters have to represent the sound of a whole word. Using letters to represent sounds is not easy; try saying the sounds in these cartoon pictures!

It is even more difficult if you try to do it yourself. For example, how would *you* write down the sounds made by each of these, just using letters?

Sounds and letters

There are 26 letters in the alphabet we use to write English:

> 21 **consonant** letters:
> **bcdfghjklmnpqrstvwxyz**
> 5 **vowel** letters: **aeiou**

One of the problems is that there are many more speech sounds in English than letters:

	Sounds	Letters
Consonants	22	20
Vowels	20	5

This is not true for all languages. For example, in Italian there are more or less the same number of sounds as there are letters. This makes it very much easier to learn to spell in Italian than in English.

Because there are more sounds than letters in English, we have to combine letters in particular ways to spell certain sounds. For example, if you see these letter combinations you know what sound to expect:

ch   sh   ng

Consonants do not cause much difficulty. The problems begin when we try to spell vowel sounds. Each of the vowel letters has to work very hard indeed. Look at the ways in which the letter **e** is used in these words:

**heart   after   date   weigh   err
pet   bear   parties   be   either
weird   sew**

English, like all modern languages that use the Roman alphabet, has two versions of each letter: large, or capital letters, and small letters.

Sometimes capital letters are called upper case letters and small letters are called lower case letters. This dates from the days when printers used cases to hold the individual pieces of type used to print books. There were separate cases for capital letters and small letters, and the case for capitals was always placed above the other.

It would be possible to write English with only one form of the letters, but we would find it difficult, because we have become accustomed to using two.

21

Getting the message across

Quite early in the history of writing, people found the need to have more than one copy of written texts. They wanted to *publish* texts, to make them public. There are many different reasons why people should want to publish their writing.

to keep a record

to entertain

to inform

Early writing
The earliest writing was done with the materials that were available: mud, wood, stone, wax.

Scrolls
The problem with these early materials is that they were not very easy to carry around. The first truly portable systems were developed with the invention of the papyrus scroll.

The disadvantage of a scroll is that it is difficult to look things up.

Books

If you cut a scroll up into sections and then join the sections together along one edge, you have a book.

Until the invention of printing, all books were handwritten. In the Middle Ages in Europe, almost all books were produced by the monasteries, so most of them were either copies of the bible or other religious books. They were often very beautiful. The people who copied out the books were called *scribes*.

Printing

Writing books out by hand was slow and often led to the introduction of mistakes into a book. Later scribes copied out the mistakes, and often added a few of their own, so that books became more and more unreliable.

The invention of printing changed all that. The Chinese developed a form of printing in the 8th and 9th centuries AD. In Europe, printing began in Germany in the 1440s. By 1510 most European books were printed rather than handwritten.

Electronic publishing

Today we are in another period of great change. More and more we are using computers and video screens to publish and read information.

4: Communicating and understanding

The time

Good morning Mrs. Hargreaves.

Hi Dave!

Who are we talking to

What is involved

The words we use, and the way in which we use them, depend on many different things.

What we are talking about

Where we are

The form of language we are using

What we are talking about

Words If you have not got the right words, it can be very difficult to explain what you mean.

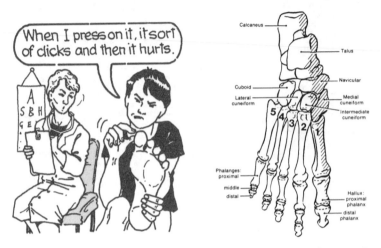

Yet even when we are talking about quite ordinary things, we have to master a large number of specialized words.

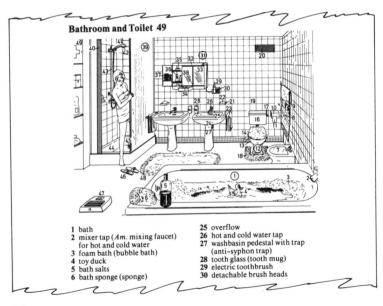

Bathroom and Toilet 49

1 bath
2 mixer tap (*Am.* mixing faucet) for hot and cold water
3 foam bath (bubble bath)
4 toy duck
5 bath salts
6 bath sponge (sponge)

25 overflow
26 hot and cold water tap
27 washbasin pedestal with trap (anti-syphon trap)
28 tooth glass (tooth mug)
29 electric toothbrush
30 detachable brush heads

Sentences Different subjects also demand different kinds of writing. The writing in a science textbook, for example, is very different from the writing in a science fiction story.

Procedure

1 Wash out five test-tubes with tap water and then distilled water. Place them in the test-tube rack.
2 One third fill the test-tubes with copper(II) sulphate solution.
3 Add lead(II) nitrate solution to the copper(II) sulphate solution until the test-tube is two-thirds full.
4 Mix the two solutions by stirring with a glass rod. Remove the glass rod. Wash it with tap water and then distilled water.
5 Record your observation in the results table.
6 Repeat steps 1–5 with potassium iodide,

I said nothing. What was there to say about Positos VI PH? The name tells you everything. The 'VI' means it's a sixth-order world — the smallest sort, the dregs. The 'P H' means 'partly hostile'. In other words, it has a tendency to kill humans. Charming.

Jargon Sometimes people use language in very complicated ways when they do not need to. They become so involved in the details of their subject matter that they forget they are trying to communicate.

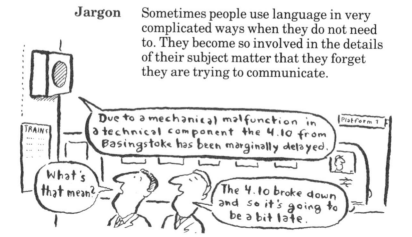

27

Who we are talking to

What goes through your mind when you have a conversation? How does it affect what you say? How does it affect what you hear and understand? You may not realize just how much thinking you do when you are talking to someone and listening to what they say.

This example is about a conversation, but similar thinking goes on when we are writing or reading. The main difference is that we have far more time to think about things. (And the reader can just stop reading, if s/he feels like it. If you stop listening to someone it is often taken as a sign of rudeness or thoughtlessness.)

When and where

Have you ever thought how much your language changes according to where you are and what time of day it is?

Getting up

On the way to school

In the classroom

On the football field

In the science lab

Part-time job

At the Youth Centre

The form of language we are using

We use language in different ways according to the particular language form we have chosen. First, of course, we choose between talking and writing. But there are many different kinds of talking and writing.

> Hullo! Well many places in Eastern Britain are in fact still dry but this pyramid of cloud here - that is racing along. You can see it coming on this morning's satellite sequence to bring rain in from the west and the south-west of Britain - rain, and there are quite strong winds in many places as well . . .
>
> (BBC TV Noon forecast 8/10/88 - Ian McGaskill).

> ...well I did listen to the weather forecast and they said it wasn't going to rain so I thought well I won't take my raincoat I haven't got a proper raincoat anyway ever since I left that nice one I got from Lewises on the train to Brighton that time...

Wednesday.
Got here yesterday — great campsite — fantastic weather — having a marvellous time!

Mel

Nick and Alison
32 Birch Grove
Oxford
OX6 4DR
England

Witnesses have testified that at the time of the attack the weather was bad, and visibility poor. "Wet and rather murky" was the way one of them described it. Members of the jury, you may well ask yourselves whether in such circumstances the key prosecution witness could have clearly identified the accused as she claims to have done...

The wind by now was more than redoubled. The shutters were bulging as if tired elephants were leaning against them, and Father was trying to tie the fastening with that handkerchief. But to push against this wind was like pushing against rock. The handkerchief, shutters, everything burst: the rain poured in like the sea into a sinking ship, the wind occupied the room, snatching pictures from the wall, sweeping the table bare. Through the gaping frames the lightning-lit scene without was visible. The creepers, which before had looked like cobwebs, now streamed up into the sky like new-combed hair. Bushes were lying flat, laid back on the ground as close as a rabbit lays back his ears.

Britons trapped as 30 die in island hurricane

AROUND 30 people were feared dead last night after Hurricane Gilbert battered Jamaica.

And 1,500 British holiday-makers were trapped on the sunshine island following what weathermen described as 'one of the worst storms this century'.

Some were taken to safe inland hotels because of fears of tidal waves: others were evacuated by air to Miami.

More than 100,000 homes have been wrecked and the country's vital banana crop destroyed. There were reports of looting in the capital, Kingston.

Damage to the Caribbean island is estimated at £117 million.

With tears in his eyes, Premier Edward Seaga said sadly: ' It's the worst natural disaster in our modern history.'

Today Hurricane Gilbert is expected to hit the gulf of Mexico. Coastal areas in Texas and Louisiana were bracing themselves for the worst as torrential rain and winds of up to 140 mph raced towards them.

The North Wind began to blow and blow and blow. People had to chase after their hats. Leaves were blown from trees. All the animals were frightened.

33

5: Vocabulary

Words and meanings

Many people take words for granted: they are what we use when we talk. They have meanings and if you are not sure of the meaning of a word you can look it up in a dictionary. But where do the meanings come from? How do we know the meanings? How can we be sure that everyone uses words to mean the same thing?

Faces If it proves difficult to describe a simple thing like a shape, it is a good deal more difficult when you come to something more interesting, like a face. A number of people were shown the three faces on this page. They were asked to write not more than six words describing each one. Opposite each face you can see some of the answers they gave.

A: "middle-aged, worn, gentle"
B: "old, haggard, worried"
C: "old, wise, kind"

A: "tired, careworn, poor"
B: "middle-aged, wrinkled, wise"
C: "grumpy, old, irritable"

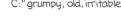

A: "smarmy, greasy, dirty"
B: "mean, foreign, calculating"
C: "refined, rich, back-stabber"

Different languages

When we compare different languages, we can see more clearly how this works. The English word 'garden' is often translated in Kiswahili (a language used in East Africa) as 'shamba'. This can be misleading.

English and Kiswahili work in different ways, because the lives of the people who speak these two languages have developed in different ways. So it is not surprising that you cannot translate exactly from one language to the other.

False friends

These differences between languages can lead to some strange situations. Words in other languages may look very much like English words, yet mean something entirely different. Such words are sometimes called false friends, because they may seem friendly but in fact they will let us down if we think they mean the same as similar English words. These are some examples:

librairie (French): bookshop
lard (French): bacon
prune (French): plum
veste (French): jacket
phrase (French): sentence

caldo (Italian): hot
also (German): therefore
constipado (Spanish): with a
head cold

Anatomy of a word

There are hundreds of thousands of words in the English language. You know and use thousands of words. If every word were completely different and separate from every other word, it would be impossible to remember anything like that number.

Word families

Words belong to families. Each has a root, from which the other members of the family can be derived. Affixes can be added before or after the root to change its meaning, or the way it can be used in sentences. Affixes that come before the root are called prefixes. Affixes that follow the root are called suffixes.

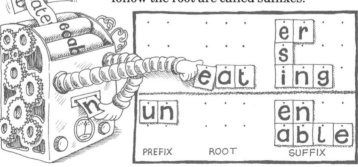

PREFIX   ROOT   SUFFIX

36

Suffixes

Suffixes are used in two main ways:

1   To change a word from one word class*
    to another:

    adjective to noun:
    bright + ness ⟶ brightness

    adjective to adverb:
    bright + ly ⟶ brightly

    adjective to verb:
    bright + en ⟶ brighten

    noun to adjective:
    child + ish ⟶ childish

    verb to noun:
    write + er ⟶ writer

    verb to adjective:
    drink + able ⟶ drinkable

2   As part of the way in which nouns,
    adjectives, and verbs inflect. Words have
    to change so that they fit the grammar of
    the sentence. For example *like* has the
    suffix -*s* added to it in this sentence:

    He likes ice cream.

    Not all words inflect just by adding a
    suffix: some common nouns and verbs
    change in other ways. For example, the
    plural of woman is women, not 'womans'.
    The past of go is went, not 'goed'.

*See page 127 on word classes.

Prefixes

The main use of prefixes is to add to the meaning of the stem, or to change it:

un + happy ⟶ unhappy
super + man ⟶ superman

If you know the commonest prefixes and what they mean, it can help you to work out the meaning of a new or unknown word.

Prefix	Meaning	Examples
ante-	before	*antedate*
anti-	against	*anti-apartheid*
arch-	big, chief	*archbishop*
auto-	self	*autograph*
bi-	two	*bicycle*
co-	joint, together	*co-operate*
contra-	opposite	*contradict*
counter-	against	*counteract*
de-	making the opposite of	*demist*
dis-	not, opposite of	*disobey*
dis-	undoing, making opposite	*disconnect*
ex-	used to be out of	*ex-soldier* *extract*
fore-	in the front of	*foreground*
fore-	before	*foretell*
hyper-	very big	*hypermarket*
in-	not, opposite of in, into	*incorrect* *insight*
inter-	between	*international*

Prefix	Meaning	Examples
mal-	bad	*malfunction*
mini-	small	*mini-computer*
mis-	wrong, false	*misprint*
mono-	one	*monochrome*
multi-	many	*multi-purpose*
neo-	new	*neo-fascist*
non-	not, opposite of	*non-smoker*
out-	beyond	*outlaw*
over-	too much	*overdone*
poly-	many	*polyhedron*
post-	after	*postpone*
pre-	before	*premature*
pro-	for	*pro-British*
re-	again back	*reprocess* *reverse*
semi-	half	*semi-conscious*
sub-	below	*submarine*
sub-	less than	*substandard*
super-	more than, special	*superman*
sur-	more than, beyond	*surpass*
trans-	across	*transport*
tri-	three	*tricycle*
ultra-	beyond	*ultraviolet*
ultra-	very much indeed	*ultra-rich*
un-	not, opposite of making opposite	*unfair* *undo*
under-	below, less than	*underpass*
uni-	one	*unicycle*

Figures of speech

When people talk or write creatively – using their imagination – they make great use of language that is not literal. Literal language is when the words mean exactly what they say – according to their dictionary definition. If someone says to you, 'I'm going to kill that bee,' then you understand clearly and literally what they mean.

But that is not the only way in which the words 'kill' and 'bee' can be used.

Figurative language

Figurative language is an important part of idiomatic speech, the language of everyday conversation:

She's always putting the cart before the horse.
He's a queer fish.
We shall leave no stone unturned in our search for your son.

Figurative language is also very important in poems, stories and advertisements.

Images We often think in images. An image is a picture that helps you to see things more clearly and describe them more vividly:

Fog drifted to school today
in a big grey ship.

Images are not just about what can be seen. As well as visual images there are also images that appeal to our other senses:

When I think of school
I hear
High shouts tossed
Like juggled balls in windy yards, and lost
In gutters, treetops, air.

As you can see from these examples, sometimes images work by providing a very vivid description, but at other times they work by comparing things, often things that are really very different.

Metaphor A metaphor is a very powerful kind of comparison. When you use a metaphor you make your readers work hard by not telling them what you are up to. You just throw the comparison at them and leave their imagination to get to work on it.

The greater-spotted brown baked bean's
not quite the humble bird it seems;
it lurks beneath the soggy greens
waiting to get you.

Simile Similes are easier, but not usually as strong. In a simile you tell people what is going on: 'In this sentence I am comparing things that are different only the same.' You do this by using words such as *like* or *as*:

High shouts tossed
Like juggled balls in windy yards.

Word books

Because there are so many words in the language, no one can know them all. So we have to use reference books to check spellings and find out meanings.

Dictionary

The commonest of these is the dictionary. If you are going to get the best value from dictionaries it is important to know how they are made and how they present information.

Modern dictionaries are produced by teams of *lexicographers* (dictionary-makers). They collect examples of how words are used in writing and in speech. Then they produce definitions based on the examples they have collected. The problem is that the language is constantly changing. New words are added and old words gradually change their meanings, or gain new meanings. This means that as soon as a dictionary is published it begins to be out of date.

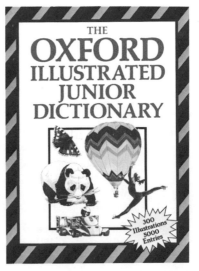

Different kinds of dictionary Not all dictionaries work by providing definitions. Some use pictures.

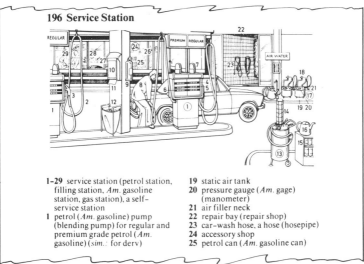

196 Service Station

1-29 service station (petrol station, filling station, *Am.* gasoline station, gas station), a self–service station
1 petrol (*Am.* gasoline) pump (blending pump) for regular and premium grade petrol (*Am.* gasoline) (*sim.:* for derv)

19 static air tank
20 pressure gauge (*Am.* gage) (manometer)
21 air filler neck
22 repair bay (repair shop)
23 car-wash hose, a hose (hosepipe)
24 accessory shop
25 petrol can (*Am.* gasoline can)

Thesaurus Sometimes you don't want to find out the meaning or spelling of a word. Instead you want to find other similar words, perhaps in order to avoid repeating the same word when you are writing, or you can't quite think of the word you want but know a word that is nearly right. Then you can use a book called a *thesaurus*. This is a collection of words grouped so that words with similar meanings are printed together. This can be done in different ways.

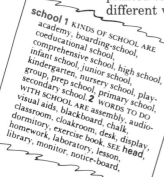

school 1 KINDS OF SCHOOL ARE academy, boarding-school, coeducational school, comprehensive school, high school, infant school, junior school, kindergarten, nursery school, play-group, prep school, primary school, secondary school. 2 WORDS TO DO WITH SCHOOL ARE assembly, audio-visual aids, blackboard, chalk, classroom, cloakroom, desk, display, dormitory, exercise book, SEE head, homework, laboratory, lesson, library, monitor, notice-board,

539 School
N. *academy*, institute, institution, educational i.; college, lycée, gymnasium, senior secondary school; conservatoire, school of music, school of dancing, ballet school, art s., academy of dramatic art; charm school, finishing school; correspondence college; university, university college; campus; Open University; redbrick university, Oxbridge, varsity; sixth-form college, college of further *or* higher education; polytechnic, poly; school of philosophy, Academy, Lyceum,

6: The structure of language

What is grammar?

The structure of language – how words work together – and the rules of this structure are called its **grammar**. When we listen to someone speaking, what we actually hear is a stream of sounds. Our knowledge of the language helps us to turn these sounds into words and sentences that make sense.

policearehuntingarazorwieldingfemalerobberwhoslashesopen
shoppingbagstostealtheircontentspolicesaythatsheslicesopen
thebagsoffemaleshoppersandthentakeschequebookscredit
cardsandcashoftenwithoutthevictimsrealisinguntilmuchlater

Words

What we say or write is composed of words. When we write, we leave spaces to show where one word ends and another begins.

police are hunting a razor wielding female robber who slashes open shopping bags to steal their contents
(Independent Radio News)

You can probably work out where the gaps come in the rest of the news broadcast.

Sentences

When we speak and write, we arrange words into sentences. In speech there are no clear divisions between sentences, although we may pause. In writing we show the beginning of a sentence with a capital letter and the end with a full stop, question mark or exclamation mark.

Police are hunting a razor-wielding female robber who slashes open shopping bags to steal their contents. Police say that she slices open the bags of female shoppers and then takes cheque-books, credit cards and cash often without the victims realising until much later.

Different kinds of grammar

There are different ways of looking at grammar. Some people see it as a scientific study.

Other people think grammar means correcting mistakes in the way people speak and write.

Who is right? The answer is that in their own ways both are right. 'I done it yesterday' is used by a lot of people when they speak. People understand them perfectly well, because they are speaking with the grammar of the area where they live. But it is not Standard English and we should normally use Standard English when we write, unless there is a good reason for using dialect.

45

Speech and writing

Some people think that talking and writing are much the same. If you listen carefully to the words and sentences that people use when they speak, *and* the pauses and noises between them, you will see that this is not true.

What they said   (– means a pause; / means a natural break in the rhythm of the speech.)

Disc Jockey: picture the scene / a ski slope in the middle of Leicester Square / and at the top with his goggles and his helmet on / Eddie the Eagle Edwards / let's face it / no one else in the world performs a ski-jump carrying a portable telephone / he's there, now / – Eddie / exactly what are you doing / – describe the scene for us /
Eddie: well I'm about forty – forty-five feet up / – I'm right in front of the – er – Empire / and – er – I'm just about to jump –

46

Disc Jockey: this is the Empire Ballroom in Leicester Square /
Eddie: right – that's right / that's where I am / and I'm just about to jump off this little ramp and land on a big mat / about ten foot tall and about twenty-four foot wide /
Disc Jockey: as I remember there's a lot of trees in that Square /
Eddie: yes – I'm jumping between the trees /
Disc Jockey: you're going in between the trees /
Eddie: that's right /
Disc Jockey: and they've erected this special ski slope so you can do it /
Eddie: yes / (BBC Radio 1)

The differences

When we speak we have the opportunity to alter what we are saying as we go along:

... well I'm about forty – forty-five feet up ...

We can refer to things that the listener will understand:

... I'm just about to jump off this little ramp ...

If we can't think of what to say we can pause, say 'er', and even go on in a different way:

I'm right in front of the – er – Empire / and – er – I'm just about to jump –

When you write you cannot keep checking to make sure that your reader has understood. So you have to be much more careful about your sentences. Similarly you cannot have the sudden changes of direction that sometimes happen in speech. As a result the grammar of written English is stricter than the grammar of spoken English.

47

Kinds of sentence

There are four main types of sentence.

Statement I've got a headache.

These are the commonest kind of sentence. Most of what we say or write is made up of statements.

Question Aren't you feeling well?

If we want to find out information we ask a question. Many questions begin with special question words, like *what*, or have a different word order from statements, or both:

Statement: You aren't feeling well.
Question: Aren't you feeling well?

Command/ request Take two of these.

If we want someone to do something we make a command or request.

Commands usually take just the simple or stem form of the verb (*take*, not *are taking*), and usually there is no subject in the sentence (although we can say that *you* is understood).

Exclamation

What a headache I've got!

Exclamations often start off with a word like *what* or *how*. They also have a different word order from statements and questions.

Statement: I've got a headache.
Question: Have I got a headache?
Exclamation: What a headache I've got!

Grammar and usage

Questions, commands and exclamations usually have different patterns from statements. In everyday speech this is not always true. By changing the way we say a sentence, we can give it a different purpose.

We can change a statement into a question or even an exclamation.
A question can become an exclamation.

How sentences work

Have you ever wondered how we manage to make up so many different sentences, without having to stop and think about each one? When you have a conversation with someone you make up sentence after sentence with only occasional pauses and ers and ums. Some of those sentences are probably brand new to you: you have never spoken that particular combination of words before. The reason we are able to do this is that sentences follow **patterns**.

Subject

Statements, questions and exclamations have a **subject**. It usually tells us *who* or *what* the sentence is about. We can see how important it is in a sentence if we miss it out.

Verb

Sentences in Standard English normally have a **verb**. It is the most important single part of a sentence, as you can see if you remove it from sentences. If the sentence is about an action or situation, then the verb helps to express the action or situation.

How many verbs?

Some sentences have just one verb:

Liverpool *won* the cup.

That well-known Merseyside football team Liverpool *won* the FA Cup in an exciting match against Everton.

Notice that sometimes quite long sentences still only have one main verb.

Other sentences have more than one verb:

When I *woke* up this morning I *heard* on the radio that Liverpool *had won* the cup and this *made* me very sad because I *have* always *been* an Everton supporter.

A sentence like this is made up of a number of sections, or *clauses*. Each one has its own verb:

When I *woke* up this morning
I *heard* on the radio
that Liverpool *had won* the cup
and this *made* me very sad
because I *have* always *been* an Everton supporter.

Clause patterns We can make up very long sentences which contain a number of clauses. The sentences themselves may be complicated, but the clauses that make them up belong to a small number of clause **patterns**. When we are learning our language we learn these patterns quite early on. Once we have learned a pattern, we can use it to make any number of sentences:

Liverpool	won	the cup.
That well-known Merseyside football team Liverpool	won	the FA Cup in an exciting match against Everton.
Dave and Hilary	are trying to catch	the first train to London.

51

7: History

Where English came from

People sometimes describe English as a mongrel language. It has certainly been influenced by many different languages and cultures. So if you want to understand where our modern language came from, you have to study the history of Britain and of the other countries where English is a major language.

A story of invasions

The Celts

The first Celtic people (the original ancient Britons) came to the British Isles in the 4th century BC. They spoke a language which developed into Gaelic. Some people in Scotland and Ireland still speak Gaelic today. Later on, Celts settled in England speaking a form of Celtic which developed into Welsh and Cornish.

The Romans

When the Romans invaded Britain, the official language of the people who governed the country was Latin. The British people still spoke Celtic. Gradually, as the Roman Empire grew weaker, Roman control of Britain declined.

The Anglo-Saxons

During the 5th century AD, Britain was invaded by people from what is now northern Germany and Denmark. They spoke a Germanic language which developed into Old English (sometimes called Anglo-Saxon). This is the basis of the language we speak today. Almost all the hundred most common modern English words come from the language of these people. After the Anglo-Saxon invasions, Celtic was largely confined to Cornwall, Wales and Scotland.

The Vikings

Lindisfarne A.D. 793
Thornaby on tees
Appleby
Whitby
Selby
Grimsby
Derby
Corby
Rugby
London
Winchester

--- The Danelaw
⟶ Direction of Viking attacks

During the eighth, ninth, tenth, and eleventh centuries, Britain was attacked by warriors from the area that is now Norway and Denmark. They gradually occupied much of North and East England. They spoke Old Norse, a language which was quite similar to the language of the Anglo-Saxons. Many words in modern English come from these Scandinavian settlers.

Where words come from		
Celtic *(very few)*	*examples:*	crag tor
Anglo-Saxon *(very many)*	*examples:*	a and is was you what day night wood town sheep earth house
Scandinavian *(very many)*	*examples:*	get hit leg want wrong sky low root

The Norman Conquest

The Normans, who conquered England in 1066, used two languages. Latin was their official language. All the documents which were produced for the King were in Latin, which was also the language of the church, so all services were in Latin. When the Normans spoke to each other, they spoke French. The ordinary people, the English, continued to speak Old English. So at this time there were no fewer than three languages being used in England.

French and English

If an Englishman wanted to make progress under the Normans he had to learn two languages: Latin and French. At the same time, if the Normans wanted to get things done, they had to learn some English. By the fourteenth century, English was being used more and more by the rich and powerful men at Court, but it was a language that was changing rapidly. French words began to come into English.

A choice of words

The result of this was that often in modern English we have a choice of words. Some come from Old English and some from Norman French; for example:
rise/ascend
get/acquire
keep/retain.

Sometimes the choice of words has meant that we now use 'English' words for one purpose and 'French' for another. Thus English words are used for animals, and French ones for the meat that we get from the animal:

English	French	
sheep	mouton	⟶ mutton
cow/bull/ox	boeuf	⟶ beef
pig/swine	porc	⟶ pork

Middle English By the fourteenth century, English had changed a lot. To a modern English speaker, Old English looks like a foreign language. If you heard it spoken, you would find it difficult to recognize any words at all. The English of 1400, which is called Middle English, looks much more like the English that we speak today. These lines come from the first part of *The Canterbury Tales* by Geoffrey Chaucer. This long poem was written at the very end of the fourteenth century. It describes a group of people who are going on a pilgrimage to the shrine of St Thomas at Canterbury. There was a miller:

His berd as any sowe or fox was reed,
And therto brood, as though it were a
*   spade.*
Upon the cop right of his nose he hade
A werte, and theron stood a toft of herys,
Reed as the brustles of a sowes erys.

(His beard was as red as a sow or a fox, and as broad as a spade. Right on the top of his nose he had a wart with a tuft of hair on it as red as the bristles in a sow's ears.)

Building the vocabulary

From the time of Chaucer onwards, English became more and more like the language we speak today. Throughout history it has taken in words from other languages, as they have been needed.

Greek Many words have been taken from Ancient Greek. Others have been invented, using words that were originally Greek. These words sometimes have an unusual spelling. This is because Greek has a number of letters that do not exist in English.

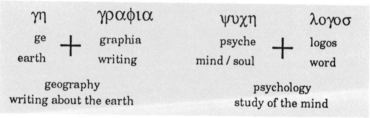

γη	γραφια	ψυχη	λογοσ
ge	graphia	psyche	logos
earth	writing	mind / soul	word

geography
writing about the earth

psychology
study of the mind

Other common Greek words used to make English words include:

phone = voice
phos/photis = light
philo = like or love
sophe = wisdom
tele = send

bi = two
tri = three
tetra = four
penta = five
poly = many

Latin Some very common English words come from Latin. Some have come directly from Latin and date from the time the Romans ruled Britain. Others have come by way of French, and others have been made up, using Latin words. Some common Latin words used in this way were:

pes/pedis = foot
videre/visum = see
  (video = 'I see')
multum/multi =
  much/many

super = above
sonus = sound
sub = under
mare = sea

Other countries

Going west

potato tomato
hickory wigwam
racoon totem
igloo kayak

squatter prairie
popcorn
backwoodsman

From the fifteenth century onwards Europeans explored the Atlantic and then the continents of America. They encountered new peoples, new ways of life, new plants and animals. They borrowed words which have found their way into our vocabulary.

As the explorers settled in North America and made their own way of life, they added words of their own.

Ever since then, America, especially the United States, has added thousands of words to the English language.

The east

Arabic: algebra
sugar assassin
zenith admiral
alcohol

India: bungalow
khaki thug
curry juggernaut
jungle verandah

From the early Middle Ages, people from the Arabic-speaking countries of the Middle East travelled west to Europe, bringing with them their ideas and their culture. Europeans explored eastwards, through the Middle East and on into India and beyond. From this two-way contact many new words came into European languages including English.

Science and technology

hypnopaedia
polystyrene
quasar

The explorers of today are the scientists and technologists of the space age. It is in science and technology that many new words are being added to English every day. Because they are words to describe new inventions and discoveries, the words, too, have to be invented.

Scientists also use old words in new ways, as in these two phrases from modern astronomy:

red dwarf   greenhouse effect

8: What kind of English?

Accent and dialect

Accent

You can often tell where people come from simply by the way they pronounce words. Many Scots say the word *house* so that it rhymes with *loose*. People from the South-East of England give it a completely different vowel sound. In the North of England the words *pass* and *pat* are usually given the same vowel sound, whereas in the South they are not. These different ways of pronouncing words are described as accents.

People often think that some speakers 'have an accent', while others do not. This is not true. Everyone has an accent of some kind, and in reality no accent is better than any other. There is, however, one particular accent which some believe is better than others. This is the southern English accent used by many BBC newsreaders. It is sometimes called Received Pronunciation (or RP, for short). Many people change between RP and their home accent according to who they are with. It is certainly important that all speakers of English should be able to understand each other. At times this means that we may have to adapt our accents so that people from different places can understand us.

Dialect There are other, and more important, differences between the forms of English used by speakers from different parts of Britain, and from different parts of the world. Not only do they pronounce the same words in different ways: they may also use different words and even different grammar to convey the same meaning.

What is dialect? The word dialect means a form of the
language used in a particular area or by a
particular group of people.

Truce words used in different
parts of the country

Standard English

Everyone uses at least one dialect and many people use more than one, according to the people they are speaking to. There is, however, one dialect of English which is much more common than the others, especially in writing. This is called Standard English. It is the version of English normally used for writing. It is also very widely used in speech, in government, business, commerce and education. Standard English is very widespread and is not tied to any particular region or group of people. As a result, many people think of it as correct and other, regional, dialects as incorrect. This is not true: there are many situations in which it would be incorrect, or at least very strange, to use Standard English rather than dialect.

The best thing is to adapt your dialect to the situation. For writing, and speaking in many formal situations, Standard English is more suitable. It is also useful when speaking to people from different parts of the world who may not understand your regional dialect. With friends and family you are much more likely to feel at home using your regional dialect.

English across the world

In many countries in the world English is the first language: the language that babies learn when they first learn to talk. In other countries it is used as a second language: a way in which people who have different first languages communicate with each other.
In many countries although English is the 'official language' (the language of government), it is not used by people in their everyday lives. Then they use their own local languages.

USSR

CHINA

PAKISTAN

BANGLADESH

BURMA

HONG KONG

INDIA

PHILIPPINES

SRI LANKA

MALAYSIA

PAPUA NEW GUINEA

C A

SUDAN

GANDA · KENYA

TANZANIA

MALAWI

ZIMBABWE

EP. OF
H AFRICA

AUSTRALIA

NEW
ZEALAND

English is the first language

Country	Number of first language speakers of English (million)
Australia	14
Canada	17
Great Britain	56
Irish Republic	3.3
New Zealand	3
South Africa	2
USA	215
Jamaica	2.3
Tobago	1.2
Other Caribbean Countries	2

Countries where English has an official status

Bangladesh	Nepal
Botswana	Nigeria
Brunei	Pakistan
Cameroon	Papua New Guinea
Fiji	Philippines
Ghana	Sierra Leone
Hong Kong	Singapore
India	Sri Lanka
Kenya	Tanzania
Lesotho	Uganda
Malawi	Zambia
Malaysia	Zimbabwe
Malta	
Mauritius	

Part B: Reading

9: Reading for information

What and how

Once you have learned to read reasonably well, it is tempting to think: 'That's all there is to it. I can read, and that's that.' In fact, there are many different kinds of reading, just as there are many different kinds of book, and many different reasons for reading them.

What kind of book? The kind of book you read affects the way you read it. Public libraries usually divide books up like this.

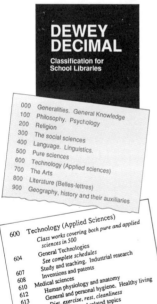

DEWEY DECIMAL
Classification for School Libraries

000	Generalities. General Knowledge
100	Philosophy. Psychology
200	Religion
300	The social sciences
400	Language. Linguistics.
500	Pure sciences
600	Technology (Applied sciences)
700	The Arts
800	Literature (Belles-lettres)
900	Geography, history and their auxiliaries

600 Technology (Applied Sciences)
Class works covering both pure and applied sciences in 500

604	General Technologies
	See complete schedules
607	Study and teaching. Industrial research
608	Inventions and patents
610	Medical sciences
612	Human physiology and anatomy
613	General and personal hygiene. Healthy living
	Diet, exercise, rest, cleanliness
614	Public health and related topics
620	Engineering and allied operations
620.1	Engineering mechanics and materials

'Fiction' is easy enough, because it means 'stories'. 'Non-fiction' includes everything else.

In fact, your local junior library is probably arranged like this:

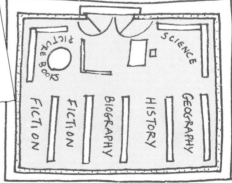

Ways of reading

There are several ways in which we can read. The most important are:

Skimming

Skimming gives you a quick picture of what a page or group of pages is about. You let your eyes skim over the page so that you get a general idea of what it is about. Titles, headings and captions provide useful clues when you are skimming. So do the first and last sentences on the page.

Sampling

You can do a similar thing with a whole chapter, or even a whole book, by dipping into it. You have a look at a number of pages to get a sample of what the book is about and how it is written. You often see people doing this when they are choosing books in the library. You can get a good idea of what an information book is like by looking at its illustrations, the table of contents, and the index.

Normal reading

This is the way in which you read when you read a story, or any other book, just for pleasure. You are not really aware of how you are reading: you read at your own fastest natural speed.

Careful reading

Sometimes you need to read more slowly. If you are reading for information and do not want to miss anything important, you may need to slow yourself down, so that you take everything in.

Reading aloud

From time to time it is useful to read aloud: for example, poems, and information or instructions that are complicated and need sorting out.

What kind of book ... what kind of reader?

What you get out of a book depends on what the writer, and *you*, put into it.

The reader. Special experience and knowledge – wants to read a particular kind of book, or get particular information.

The writer. Special experience and knowledge – wants to write a particular kind of book.

The first thing to understand is what *kind* of book you are reading.

The Outback

These four pieces of writing are all about the Australian Outback. As you read them you will be able to see the writers' different experience and knowledge of the Outback. You should also be able to see that each sets out to write a very different kind of book.

Any trip into the remote Outback cannot be undertaken lightly: four wheel drive vehicles fitted out with spare parts, water tanks and extra fuel are essential for any trips off the principal long distance routes. Secondary tracks often peter out and it is easy to become lost in the featureless scrub and spinifex (spiky grass). The earth can get so hot that it burns through rubber-soled shoes.

A large water bottle and sun hat are essential pieces of equipment. Water is a precious commodity in places where the time between rainfalls is measured in years rather than days, and it should never be squandered. On drought-stricken properties, it is not unusual for bath water to be recycled for laundry and for showers to be rationed.

The bush boy led the way hesitatingly: across the salt-pans, through the scattered yellow-jackets - poor relations to the gums - around the outcrop of quartz and granite. It was eight years since his tribe had last passed this way. He'd been little more than a toddler then; but small as he was his memory and instinct had been at work, recording land-marks, storing up information that might be of use for the future - information that was proving invaluable now.

Soon they came to a valley, gently-rising, coiling like a lifeless snake aslant a range of low granite hills.

Northern Territory
The Northern Territory covers an area of 519,633 square miles. It occupies 17.5 per cent of the whole continent. It is two and a half times the size of France and six times the size of Britain. The distance between its Northern and Southern extremities is the distance between London and Lisbon or between New York and Miami.

At Mongrel Downs beyond the Tanami Desert, a girl of nine receives by two-way radio an English lesson from the School of the Air in Alice Springs, seven hundred kilometres away along a red dust track. At a place called Utopia, the Aboriginal Land Commissioner listens to a Pitjantjara man claim, in the words of the Land Rights Act, 'primary spiritual responsibility for the site'. Above the Barkly Tablelands, a flying doctor makes a final approach to a dirt airstrip marked with forty-four-gallon drums painted white. By the strip, in the back of a truck, lies a twenty-two-year-old stockman whose ankle has been crushed by a Land-Rover which rolled while he was chasing a wild bull.

Information books

Information books often contain a lot of illustrations: photographs, drawings and diagrams, as well as the text you read. Sometimes this means that the pages are organized in a complicated way, as you can see from the example.

Main text
This contains the main factual information on the page.

Taste

There are small groups of receptor cells in your tongue, called **taste buds.** Certain chemicals in food dissolve in the saliva in the mouth and stimulate these cells so that you can distinguish different tastes. Information about taste travels to the brain via sensory nerve cells and is dealt with by a special area of the cortex.

There are four basic tastes – bitter, sweet, sour and salty. Different taste buds are sensitive to different kinds of taste. However, the various types of taste bud are not evenly distributed over your tongue. This means that some areas of the tongue are more sensitive to certain kinds of taste than others.

Your senses of taste and smell work closely together. If you cannot smell properly, for example when you have a blocked nose because of a cold, you may also find that you cannot taste properly either.

Labelled diagram
This 'backs up' the main text.

THE TONGUE

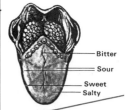

- Bitter
- Sour
- Sweet
- Salty

The taste buds on different parts of your tongue respond to different tastes.

The back of the tongue is particularly sensitive to bitter tastes, while the front and sides respond more to sweet and sour tastes. The middle of the tongue responds to salty tastes.

The taste buds are around the base of the tiny bumps that you can see all over the surface of your tongue.

Additional information
More details to add to the main text.

✳ With training, people can learn to distinguish many more tastes than is normal. Two examples of people who use this skill are tea and wine tasters.

✳ You also have taste buds on the root of your tongue and in the soft part of the back of the roof of your mouth.

✳ As a person grows older, they have fewer taste buds and so become less sensitive to taste.

Other things it's interesting to know

Reading You can read a page like this in different ways:

- Just let your eyes wander over it, stopping at the parts you find interesting.
- Look at the pictures and diagrams to get an idea of what the page is about.
- Read the text first to get the main information and then look at the other things on the page.
- Search the page for the particular piece of information you need.

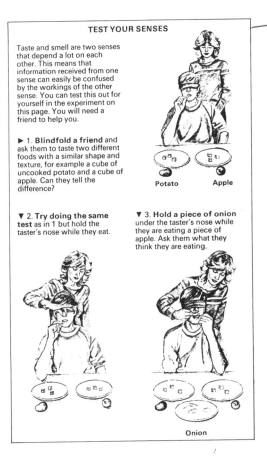

TEST YOUR SENSES

Taste and smell are two senses that depend a lot on each other. This means that information received from one sense can easily be confused by the workings of the other sense. You can test this out for yourself in the experiment on this page. You will need a friend to help you.

▶ 1. **Blindfold a friend** and ask them to taste two different foods with a similar shape and texture, for example a cube of uncooked potato and a cube of apple. Can they tell the difference?

Potato   Apple

▼ 2. **Try doing the same test** as in 1 but hold the taster's nose while they eat.

▼ 3. **Hold a piece of onion** under the taster's nose while they are eating a piece of apple. Ask them what they think they are eating.

Onion

Things to do
To help you understand in a practical way.

71

Getting information from different places

A lot the of reading we do in everyday life is for information. Often we have to look in several different places to find the information we need. This may mean studying different types of reading material.

Visit to London

Suppose you have decided to spend a day in London. You want to visit the Christmas Home Computer Show in the morning; in the afternoon you are thinking of going to either the Tower of London or the Guinness World of Records exhibition. These are some of the things you might need to read while planning your day. How would you organize the trip?

THE

CHRISTMAS

HOME COMPUTER SHOW

Olympia, Kensington
December 5-7th
10am - 6pm

All makes
Competitions
Demonstrations
Computer Games

Entry fee £2.50 adult £1 child

Nearest tube: High Street Kensington

Tower of London. 2D73
Built in part by William the Conqueror in 1078 as a fortress to guard the river approach to London, this is the most perfect example of a medieval castle in England, the outer walls being added later. The White Tower contains, besides its collection of firearms and execution relics, the finest early-Norman chapel in this country. The Crown Jewels are housed in Waterloo Block. Heralds Museum shows history and development of heraldry. Wall Walk gives good views over the Tower and River. Anne Boleyn, Katherine Howard, Lady Jane Grey, Margaret Countess of Salisbury, Jane Viscountess Rochford, Robert Devereux Earl of Essex, were executed on Tower Green.
Admission Charge extra charge for the Jewel House. Weekdays March to end October 9.30 a.m. to 5 p.m. November to end February 9.30 a.m. to 4 p.m. Sundays 2 p.m. to 5 p.m. March to end October. Closed Good Friday, Christmas Day and Boxing Day, New Year's Day. Jewel House closed all Feb. for cleaning.
Station: Tower Hill Cir.D.

Trafalgar Square. 2C69
Laid out as a war memorial and named after the victory of Trafalgar, the Square was completed in 1841. In the centre ... exhibitions: Open Mon. to Sat. 10 a.m. to 5 p.m.; Sun.: (May to Sept.) 2 to 5 p.m.
Station: Bank Cen N. & SR.

Guinness World of Records, Trocadero Centre, Piccadilly Circus. 1B 68
An exhibition designed to transform the 'Book of Records' into an exciting three-dimensional presentation. Admission charge. Open 10 a.m. to 10 p.m. daily. Closed Xmas Day.
Station: Piccadilly Circus

Hampton Court Palace, see page 38.
Hatton Garden, Holborn. 2B60
Stands partly on the site of the old palace of the Bishop of

Making notes

When you are reading for information or ideas, you may need to make notes, especially if you are working on a number of books – in a library, for example. There are different ways in which you can do this.

Lists You can make a list of the main points you want to remember.

Crustaceans: crabs
lobsters
shrimps
prawns

Key words and details You can pick out the key words in what you are reading. Use them as headings and then add any details you want to remember. If you use a different colour for the key words, it makes your notes clearer and easier to use.

SOLAR HEAT FOR ELECTRICITY

A) Solar furnace mirrors focus sun's rays onto one point
heat used to produce steam.

B) Solar pond salt water in shallow pool heats up
used to heat fresh water
fresh water heated more to produce steam.

Labelled diagram Sometimes the best way to record information is to use a labelled diagram.

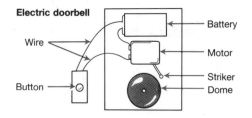

Electric doorbell

Wire

Button

Battery

Motor

Striker
Dome

Web diagram A web diagram also uses key words or key ideas, but you write them down in a different way.

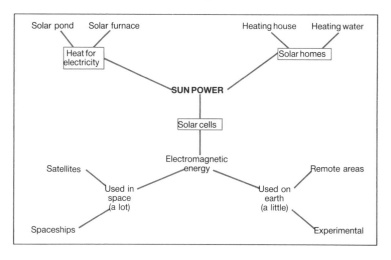

Flow chart If you are making notes on a *process*, something that happens, or how to do something, then a flow chart is a good way to make notes.

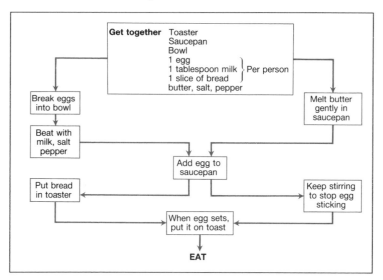

75

Using a dictionary

A dictionary is one of the most useful reference books there is. But if you are to get the most help from your dictionary, you must know how to use it.

First word — **beverage**

Parts of speech

29

Last word — **bind**

horizontal or vertical; tool for making bevels. v. (p.t. *bevelled*), give bevel to; slant.
beverage (bev-er-ij) *n.* any kind of drink.
bevy (bev-i) *n.* a company or gathering.
bewail *v.t.* wail over, mourn for.
beware *v.* (only in imper. & inf.) be cautious (*of*), be on one's guard.
bewilder *v.t.* confuse, puzzle. **bewildering** *adj.* **bewilderment** *n.*
bewitch *v.t.* put a magic spell on; delight. **bewitching** *adj.*
bey *n.* (Hist.) Turkish governor.
beyond *adv.* at or to the further side; further on. *prep.* at or to the further side of; later than; more than; except. *n.* life after death, the unknown.
bezel (bez-ël) *n.* sloped edge of chisel, etc.; groove for watch-glass, etc.
bezique (biz-**eek**) *n.* card-game for two.
bi- *pref.* twice; having two; occurring or appearing once in every two.
biannual *adj.* occurring twice a year.
bias *n.* inclination, leaning; prejudice; (in game of bowls) curved course of bowl due to its shape. *on the bias*, (Dressmaking) diagonally across fabric. *v.* give bias to; prejudice.
bib *n.* cloth placed under child's chin to protect clothing; top of apron or overalls.
Bible *n.* sacred writings of the Christian faith; sacred book. **biblical** *adj.* of the Bible.
bibliography (bib-li-og-rā-fi) *n.* history of books; list of books of any author, subject, etc. **bibliographer** (bib-li-og-rā-fer) *n.* **bibliographic(al)** (bib-li-ō-**graf**-ik-āl) *adj.*
bibliophile (**bib**-li-ō-fyl) *n.* book-lover.
bibulous *adj.* addicted to alcoholic drink.
bicarbonate *n.* salt of carbonic acid in which metal replaces only one hydrogen atom. **bicarbonate (of soda)**, sodium bicarbonate, used in cookery, medicine, etc.
bicentenary (by-sen-**teen**-er-i) *adj.* & *n.* (of) the 200th anniversary or its celebration.
biceps (by-seps) *n.* muscle with double head or attachment. (pl. **biceps**), that at front of upper arm.
bicker *v.i.* quarrel, squabble.
bicuspid (by-**kusp**-id) *adj.* & *n.* two-cusped (tooth).
bicycle *n.* two-wheeled pedal-driven vehicle. *v.i.* ride on bicycle.

Head word — **bid**

bid *v.* (p.t. *bade, bid*; p.p. *bidden, bid*), command (p.t. *bade*); invite (p.t. *bade*); offer (price), make bid at bridge (p.t. *bid*). *n.* offer of price; (Bridge) statement of number of tricks one hopes to make. **biddable** *adj.* obedient. **bidding** *n.* command; offers at auction; bids at bridge.
bide *v. bide one's time*, await one's opportunity.
bidet (bee-day) *n.* low basin which can be sat on for washing lower parts of body.
biennial (by-en-i-āl) *adj.* occurring every two years; lasting two years. *n.* plant that lives two years and flowers in second year.
bier *n.* movable stand on which coffin is placed.
bifocal (by-**foh**-kāl) *adj.* (of spectacle lenses) with two parts, for distant and near vision. **bifocals** (by-**foh**-kālz) *n.pl.* bifocal spectacles.

bifurcate (by-fer-kayt) *v.* divide into two branches; fork. **bifurcation** *n.*
big (*adj.*) (bigger, biggest), large; grown-up; important; boastful. **bigwig** *n.* (*informal*) important person.
bigamy (big-ā-mi) *n.* second marriage while first is still valid. **bigamist** *n.* **bigamous** *adj.*
bight (*rhymes with* kite) *n.* loop of rope; curve, recess, of coast, river, etc.
bigot (big-öt) *n.* person who holds obstinately or unreasonably to a creed or opinion. **bigoted** *adj.* **bigotry** (big-öt-ri) *n.*
bike *n.* & *v.i.* (*informal*) bicycle.
bikini *n.* woman's scanty two-piece bathing-suit.
bilateral (by-lat-er-āl) *adj.* of, on, with, two sides; between two parties.

Pronunciation

bilberry *n.* dwarf shrub of heaths, etc.; its deep-blue edible fruit; whortleberry.
bile *n.* bitter fluid secreted by the liver to aid digestion; anger, peevishness.
bilge (bilj) *n.* nearly horizontal part of ship's bottom; (also *bilge-water*) foul water that collects in bilge; (*slang*) nonsense, rot.
bilingual (by-ling-wāl) *adj.* in or speaking two languages.
bilious (bil-yūs) *adj.* caused by, affected by, disorder of the bile.
bilk *v.t.* avoid payment of (creditor, bill); cheat, esp. by running away.
bill¹ *n.* bird's beak; narrow promontory. *v.i.* (of doves) stroke bill with bill. *bill and coo*, exchange caresses.
bill² *n.* draft of proposed Act of Parliament; note of charges for goods, work done, etc.; poster. *v.t.* announce on poster. **billposter, billsticker** person who pastes up posters, etc.

Related words

billabong *n.* (Austral.) branch of river forming backwater or stagnant pool.
billet *n.* place where soldier, etc., is lodged. *v.t.* quarter (soldiers, etc., on town, etc.). **billetee** *n.* person billeted.
billet-doux (bil-ay-doo) *n.* (pl. *billets-doux*, pr. bil-ay-doo), love-letter.
billhook *n.* implement for pruning.
billiards *n.* game played with cues and balls on cloth-covered table (*billiard-ball, -cue, -table*).
billingsgate *n.* abusive language (as spoken in *Billingsgate* fish-market in 17th c.).
billion *n.* a million millions; (chiefly U.S. and Canada) a thousand millions.
billow *n.* great wave. *v.i.* rise or move in billows. **billowy** *adj.*
billy, billy-can *n.* tin can with (lid and) wire handle used as kettle, etc., in camping.
billy-goat *n.* male goat.
bin *n.* container for corn, coal, bread, etc.; receptacle for rubbish.
binary (by-ner-i) *a.* of two, dual; (Math.) of scale, system) with two, not ten, as base of notation. **binary digit**, one of two digits (0 and 1) in a binary system of notation.
bind *v.* (p.t. & p.p. *bound*), tie, fasten, attach; fasten or hold together; edge with tape, etc.; impose obligation on; fasten (sheets of book) into

Definition

Alpabetical order	Words in a dictionary are listed in alphabetical order.
First and last words	These are printed at the top of each page. They help you find the page you are looking for.
Head word	This is the word to which all the other words in that entry are linked. For example, *happily* and *happiness* will be found under the head word *happy*. Words that change as we use them in sentences are always shown in their stem or base form. So you should not look for *buying*, *buys*, or *bought* in a dictionary. You should look for *buy*.
Word class	This is explained on page 127. It helps you understand how the word can be used in sentences.
Pronunciation	Some dictionaries give the pronunciations of all words; some just give the difficult ones. It is a good idea to learn the system that your dictionary uses to show how words are pronounced.
Definition	Notice that some words have more than one meaning. These are numbered to show where one ends and another begins.
Related words	Words that are closely related to the head word are listed after it. These include derivations (for example, an adverb that can be made from an adjective) and compound words that contain the head word.
Derivation	Some dictionaries tell you where a word comes from.
Alphabet order games	On page 167 there is a game which will help you to use alphabetical order.

10: Reading literature

Reading a story

As you read a story, your mind is working in all sorts of different ways. When you look back on the story afterwards, or talk to someone else about it, you may sort out some of the things your mind has been working on.

People

Stories are usually about people (or animals who seem to behave like people). So it's important to get a clear idea of what the people are like. For example in the story opposite:

What does John look like? How does he behave?

Setting

As you read you begin to understand the setting of the story: where and when it takes place. Sometimes the author tells you directly: 'Farmer Woolley's field, the twelve acre has two ponds in it.' In other stories, like the one opposite, you have to pick up clues:...the school register...; ... no one at school...It is easy to work out where the story is set, but other questions come into your mind: 'What kind of school? How long ago?' So, as you read, you keep your eyes open for more clues.

Talking

There are stories that contain no speech at all. Most contain some, and many contain a lot. Conversations push the story along in different ways:
● they tell us about characters and their relationships (how they get on together).
● They tell us about actions.
● They tell us about characters' thoughts.

Action

Every story contains action. The reader visualises the action, seeing what happens in her mind's eye.

● Some of the *actions are background:* _____

● Some are *key points in the story:*

As well as imagining actions, the reader thinks about their importance.
Why is it important that John had two black eyes?
What is odd about it?
How could it have happened?

His name was John Dafte, or as the school register put it, Dafte John. No one made jokes about it. He was a tall, hairy boy, with huge shoulders and long arms and a voice like a big drum. Junior boxing champion, captain of both the cricket and football teams - there wasn't a sport he didn't excel at. We called him, respectfully, Prince Kong. I admired him tremendously. He was a smiling, good-natured hero, with a strong sense of fair play. He had only to stroll out onto the playground for the bullies to crawl back into their holes.
'Pick on someone your own size,' he'd say. It must have limited his choice: there was no one at school anywhere near his size. He dwarfed even the masters. I thought him a true prince. It didn't worry me that he looked like a gorilla. I like gorillas. On the Monday morning after half term, he came to school with two black eyes, and a split and swollen nose, decorated with dark scabs like beetles. We crowded round him sympathetically. 'Hey, Prince, you got dark glasses on?' ''Ad an argument with a bulldozer, 'ave you?' 'Your mum been beating you up?' I was not as surprised as the others that he should have come off worst in a fight. I'm good at maths, and can work out that it's no use having the strength of ten, if you happen to pick a quarrel with eleven. It would be just like Prince Kong, I thought, to go charging in to save someone from a gang of toughs, without stopping to count; what did puzzle me was that he should lie about it. I'd have expected him to smile and say, 'Can't win 'em all.' Something like that. Instead he shouldered us roughly out of his way, his head down, his eyes furtive, muttering furiously. 'Walked into a door.' 'Poor old door, it didn't stand a chance,' I said, and wished I hadn't when he glared at me. 'Sorry, Prince,' I said hastily, stepping back. I am thin and, like glass, very breakable.
We watched him limp into the school building, and followed at a safe distance, puzzled and a little dismayed.

Reading a playscript

Plays are written to be acted. A play-script is a set of instructions for an actor: what to say, how to say it, and what to do. Playscripts also contain instructions for other people in the theatre and TV: the director, who organises the production, the designer, who designs the settings, and so on.

Setting
As you read a script you should try to 'see' what is happening, in your imagination. To do this you must have a clear idea of where it is happening. So read this part of the script carefully and make sure you understand what it means.

Action
What is happening on stage or screen is described in stage directions. Even when no action is described, there are things happening. For example, in the script extract opposite, the Doctor is 'sitting behind a table' for the rest of the conversation. But what is she doing? Can you work it out from the way the conversation goes?

Character
It is important to have a clear idea about the characters: ● what they look like ● how they move ● how they speak.

The script sometimes gives you this information in stage directions: 'She is an elderly woman who walks with a stick and speaks quietly.' At other times you have to work it out. You should be able to get an idea of what the doctor is like from this extract opposite.

Seeing the whole picture
The real skill when reading a play is to 'see' all these elements - the setting, the characters, the action - at the same time. That takes practice, and the experience of watching plays on TV and in the theatre.

Scene: *At one side of the stage - a doctor's waiting room. It is filled with an assortment of miserable - looking patients, coughing, wheezing, sneezing and moaning. Amongst them sit **Mr** and **Mrs Fraser** and their son **Ernie.***

Ernie: *[to audience, after a second]:* If you ever want to feel ill - just go and spend a happy half-hour in a doctor's waiting room. If you're not ill when you get there, you will be when you leave.

Receptionist: *[A man enters, having seen the doctor. He is moaning. He crosses the waiting room and goes out. The other patients look at him and sorrowfully shake their heads. The receptionist enters]*

Receptionist Mr and Mrs Fraser... *[**Mum** and **Dad** rise]* Doctor will see you now.

Mum: Thank you. Come on Ernie.

*[**Mum** and **Dad** and **Ernie** follow the receptionist across the stage to the **Doctor** who sits behind a table]*

Mum: Morning, Doctor.

*[**Receptionist** leaves]*

Doctor: Ah. Ah. Mr and Mrs Fraser. Is that it?

Mum: That's right. I'm Mrs Fraser...and this is my husband, Mr Fraser...and this is our son...Ernie.

Doctor: Ah, yes. Ernie. I've been hearing all sorts of things about you, young Ernie. Now, what have you been up to, eh?

Dad: Illucinations.

Doctor: I beg your pardon?

Dad: Illucinations.

Doctor: Oh, yes, illuci-quite, yes.

Mum: What my husband means doctor is that Ernie has been creating these illusions.

Doctor: Ah.

Mum: Well, they're more than illusions, really.

Dad: I'll say.

Doctor: Beg pardon?

Dad: I'll say.

Mum: He's been causing that much trouble. At school, at home, everywhere he goes. I mean we can't go on like this. His Dad's not as strong as he was, are you,Albert?

Dad: No.

Doctor: What?

Dad: No.

Doctor: Perhaps it would be better if you told me a little more about it.

Reading a poem

Getting the picture

On your first reading of the poem, try to get a picture of what it is about. Does it tell a story? Is it about thoughts? What are your first impressions on reading the poem: how did it make you feel? Are there any problems - things to think about or work out next time you read it?

Listening to the sounds

If you read the poem aloud, you will hear the sounds it makes.

Rhythm

Some poems have a regular beat. In others the rhythm is less obvious, but still important. When you read this line: ___ the word 'spite' stands out. If the line had been different: ' That spiteful regiment behind the shed' it wouldn't have worked in the same way.

Rhyme

Not all poems rhyme, but this one does. It seems to have two main effects ● it holds the poem together by giving it a pattern ● it emphasises the words that rhyme.

Sounds

Some words sound like what they describe. Such words are called onomatopoeic and add to the richness of the picture the poem produces in our minds.

Looking at the images

Poems produce pictures in our minds by describing things directly: —————— They also use comparisons, they describe things as if they were other things: '...those green spears' '...regiment of spite...' The nettles are an enemy army against whom the small boy has had to fight (and will have to fight again). Images like this are called metaphors. If the poet tells us that a comparison is being made by using 'like' or 'as' then it is called a simile.

Further in The sounds and images of the poem will gradually have their effect and become clearer as you read the poem a second and third time. It may also happen that you begin to think more deeply about it. The last line 'My son would often feel sharp wounds again' may set you thinking. It means the nettles of course - he will be stung by nettles again. But perhaps it means more than that. The father, more experienced in life than his three-year-old son knows of other 'sharp wounds' that he will 'often feel' as he grows up. So perhaps the nettles aren't just nettles after all. Perhaps they stand for the problems and pains that people have to face as they go through life. We can 'hone the blade of the hook' and 'slash them in fury' but we know that they will come back again.

Nettles

My son aged three fell in the nettle bed.
'Bed' seemed a curious name for those
    green spears,
That regiment of spite behind the shed:
It was no place for rest. With sobs and tears
The boy came seeking comfort and I saw
White blisters beaded on his tender skin.
We soothed him till his pain was not so raw.
At last he offered us a watery grin,
And then I took my hook and honed the blade
And went outside and slashed in fury with it
Till not a nettle in that fierce parade
Stood upright anymore. Next task: I lit
A funeral pyre to burn the fallen dead.
But in two weeks the busy sun and rain
Had called up tall recruits behind the shed:
My son would often feel sharp wounds again.

Vernon Scannell

Part C: Writing

11: Writing

Why write?

Most of the time when you write something, you probably do not think a lot about it – you just get on and write. But sometimes, if you begin by asking yourself a few questions, you will find that you write better.

You can have many different reasons for wanting to write something down. You may even change your reasons as you write. But it is useful to begin with some idea of *why* you are writing.

To sort things out These are examples of some of the reasons why people write.

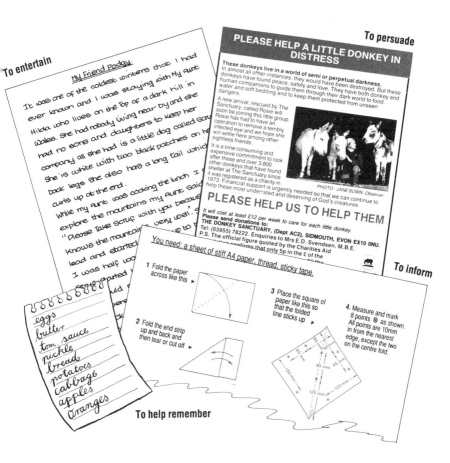

To entertain

My Friend Poday

It was one of the coldest winters that I had ever known and I was staying with my Aunt Hilda who lives on the top of a dark hill in Wales. She had nobody living near by and she had no sons and daughters to keep her company all she had is a little dog called Scru. She is white with two black patches on he back legs she also has a long tail which curls up at the end.

While my Aunt was cooking the lunch I explore the mountains my Aunt said "Please take Scrup with you because she knows the mountains very well." so I lead and started

I was half wa...

To persuade

PLEASE HELP A LITTLE DONKEY IN DISTRESS

These donkeys live in a world of semi or perpetual darkness. In almost all other instances, they would have been destroyed. But these donkeys have found peace, safety and love. They have both donkey and human companions to guide them through their dark world to food, water and soft bedding and to keep them protected from unseen dangers.

A new arrival, rescued by The Sanctuary, called Rosie will soon be joining this little group. Rosie has had to have an operation to remove a terribly infected eye and we hope she will settle here among other sightless friends.

It is a time consuming and expensive commitment to look after these and over 3,800 other donkeys that have found shelter at The Sanctuary since it was registered as a charity in 1973. Financial support is urgently needed so that we can continue to help these most underrated and deserving of God's creatures.

PHOTO - JANE BOWN. Observer

PLEASE HELP US TO HELP THEM

It will cost at least £12 per week to care for each little donkey. **Please send donations to:** **THE DONKEY SANCTUARY, (Dept AC2), SIDMOUTH, EVON EX10 0NU.** Tel: (03955) 78222. Enquiries to Mrs E.D. Svendsen, M.B.E. P.S. The official figure quoted by the Charities Aid ...that only 5p in the £ of the

To inform

You need: a sheet of stiff A4 paper, thread, sticky tape.

1 Fold the paper across like this

2 Fold the end strip up and back and then tear or cut off ►

3 Place the square of paper like this so that the folded line sticks up ►

4. Measure and mark 8 points ⊗ as shown. All points are 10mm in from the nearest edge, except the two on the centre fold.

90 mm 90 mm
65 mm 65 mm
120 mm 120 mm
85 mm
125 mm

To help remember

eggs
butter
tom. sauce
pickle
bread
potatoes
cabbage
apples
oranges

Checklist When you are planning what you are going to write, it can be useful to make some written notes.

87

A sense of audience

When you write anything that you want to be read by someone else, you should try to keep that reader in your mind. Sometimes this is easy: if you are writing for one person whom you know well. At other times it is much more difficult, because you have no clear idea of who will read what you are writing. Even then you should try to imagine the kind of person who is likely to read it.

How well do I know them?	The way in which you write depends on how well you know the person you are writing for. If it is for a friend or a member of the family you can write in a relaxed and casual way. You can use a written version of the way you speak to them. If it is for someone whom you have never met, then you will need to be more formal.
What effect do I want to have on them?	The way in which you write will affect how your reader feels about you and your subject. You may wish to have all sorts of different effects:

- to please,
- to anger,
- to make the reader sympathize.

You may affect people in ways that you do not intend. For example, if your reader is someone who is very fussy about spelling and handwriting, and you write and spell badly, then you are likely to make your reader annoyed.

How can I help them?

You also need to remember that your reader has to make sense of what you are writing. You can help by thinking about the reader's knowledge and experience. Does s/he know much about this subject, or do you need to provide some explanations? If you are writing for someone younger than you, is your writing too difficult? On the other hand, are you making it all so easy that the reader will get bored, or be offended?

'… with some sticky-back tape. Not too much! Now you should have a little piece of string left over. Take it in your right hand, very carefully…'

A sense of purpose

Most people like reading stories, and many people enjoy writing them. Sometimes you will know exactly what you want to write and how you want to write it. At other times you may not know where to start, or you may find that all your stories end up much the same. If that happens, then you may find it useful to think about some of these points.

Starting points

'How do I get ideas for my story? I can't think of anything to write.'

Many of the best ideas for stories come from things that happen in the writer's own life. They may be quite small things: a place, a face, something they overhear in the street. Then the writer's mind gets to work on it and a story starts to form.

The thing to do is to start your mind working on this *when* you see or hear something interesting, and not wait until you are sitting in front of a blank piece of paper wondering what to write.

People

Almost all stories, except for some animal stories and science fiction, are about people. One way of making up a story is to take a person (for example, your grandmother) and imagine them in a totally new situation (for example, exploring an unknown jungle).

But how do you invent people for stories? Most writers find that they start by observing real people and then add ideas of their own until they end up with a made-up character. It helps if you give your characters good names. Charles Dickens was a master at this. You only have to read the names of some of his characters to start imagining what they are like: Uriah Heep, Martin Chuzzlewit.

Who is telling the story?	Is it an 'I' story or a 'he/she' story? In an 'I' story, you take part in the story and tell it as if you were there. So you can just 'talk' to the reader naturally, but you can only describe things which *you* have actually seen or been told about. In a he/she story you can jump from one place to another, but it may be more difficult to keep the reader's interest.
Conversation	People spend a lot of time talking to each other, and conversation helps to make the story come alive. However if you have too much conversation, the story may become difficult to follow. Avoid including long conversations in which nobody says anything important. Conversations should be there for a reason.
The motor	Good stories usually have something which starts them up and keeps them going. It may be a problem that the central character has to solve. ('Will Sarah find her missing brother?') It may be something in a relationship between people. ('The family has fallen out over Jim's new girlfriend'). It may be some kind of contest. ('Will the netball team overcome injuries in time to win the cup?') The motor is what makes the reader curious to find out what happens next.
The beginning and the end	The first two or three sentences of a story are very important. If you can catch hold of the reader in those first few lines, then you are half-way there.
	It is also important to have the right ending. This may be a *twist*: the reader has been expecting the story to end in one way and then suddenly it ends in a completely different way. On the other hand, it may be a few sentences that round the story off and bring it to an end.

Explaining

One of the commonest ways in which we use written language is to *explain* things.

along the 4431 until you reach the second set of traffic lights. Turn left (the road is called Mill Lane) and continue until you reach the Gateway store. Just after it, on the right is Burton Avenue. Then it gets a bit tricky!

THE PLAY:
1. The first player combines two or more of their letters to form a word and places them on the board to read either across or down with one letter on the centre ★ square. Diagonal words are not permitted.
2. A player completes their turn by counting and announcing their score for the turn. They then draw as many new letters as they have played, thus always keeping seven letters in their rack.
3. Play passes to the left. The second player, and then each in turn, adds one or more letters to those already played so as to form new words. All letters played in any one turn must be placed in one row across or down the board. They must form one complete word and if, at the same time, they touch other letters in adjacent rows, they must form complete words, cross-word fashion, with all such letters. The player gets full credit for all words formed or modified by their play.

Checklist

Before you start this kind of writing, there are some questions you should ask yourself:

- Who am I writing for?
- How much does my reader know about this subject?
- How much can I miss out?
- What does the reader want this information for? (for example, to understand something better, to be able to do something.)
- How will my writing be used?
- Is there anything I can use to help my reader? (for example, things to look at, drawings.)

Persuading and arguing

er mother's eyes,
er father's nose,
ut where did
he get the
heart defect?

The more you help us, the more we'll find out.

Here's how you can help us in our work:
Please send this coupon to: The BHF, 102 Gloucester Place,
London W1H 4DH. Or ring 01-200 0200.

Please send me information ☐ Please send me details of
on the work of the BHF   how to leave a legacy ☐

I'm enclosing a donation ☐

Name
Address
Postcode

R/TL/5.23

British Heart Foundation
The heart research charity.

Dear Sir/Madam,

I am writing to persuade you not to stop the No. 11 bus route. This is the only bus route which goes between Heatherton and Huddersfield, and is the only means of transport for many of those who live in Heatherton.

Old people will suffer if this bus is axed, as it provides their link with shops, doctors and relatives.

When and why?

There are many different situations in which you might write in this way:

- for personal reasons (to get someone you know to do what you want, for example).
- to persuade people to agree with your point of view about an issue (for example, about cruelty to animals).
- to persuade other people to do something (for example, to join a football team, or to buy something you are selling).

What about your reader?

How much does s/he know about this subject, and so how much do you need to explain about it?

What will his/her attitude be (neutral? hostile? friendly?) and so how hard will you have to work to persuade him/her?

Reasons

The best way to persuade people, or to present an argument, is to give good reasons. Why should your reader agree with you, or do what you want? They must be reasons that you believe in *and* that your reader will find convincing.

93

Writing letters

How to set out a letter

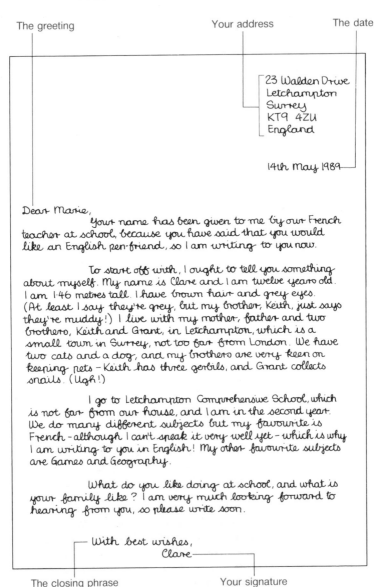

The greeting

Your address

The date

23 Walden Drive
Letchampton
Surrey
KT9 4ZU
England

14th May 1989

Dear Marie,
　　　　　Your name has been given to me by our French teacher at school, because you have said that you would like an English pen-friend, so I am writing to you now.

　　　　　To start off with, I ought to tell you something about myself. My name is Clare and I am twelve years old. I am 1·46 metres tall. I have brown hair and grey eyes. (At least I say they're grey, but my brother, Keith, just says they're muddy!) I live with my mother, father and two brothers, Keith and Grant, in Letchampton, which is a small town in Surrey, not too far from London. We have two cats and a dog, and my brothers are very keen on keeping pets – Keith has three gerbils, and Grant collects snails. (Ugh!)

　　　　　I go to Letchampton Comprehensive School, which is not far from our house, and I am in the second year. We do many different subjects but my favourite is French – although I can't speak it very well yet – which is why I am writing to you in English! My other favourite subjects are Games and Geography.

　　　　　What do you like doing at school, and what is your family like? I am very much looking forward to hearing from you, so please write soon.

　　　　　With best wishes,
　　　　　　　　Clare

The closing phrase

Your signature

Your address	People usually start a letter with their full address, although it is not really necessary if you are writing to a friend or a member of the family, who knows it already.
The date	You can write it in full, as in the example; or, when writing to friends or family, use a shorter form, for example, Tuesday, or Tuesday 3rd May.
The greeting and the closing phrase	The most widely-used ones are: To people you do not know at all: *Dear Sir or Madam,* *Yours faithfully,* *A.B. Carter* To people you know a little: *Dear Mr/Mrs/Miss/Ms* _____ *Yours sincerely,* *Anne Carter* To friends: *Dear + first name* (The ending depends on how well you know them.)
The envelope	When you address an envelope make sure that the address is in the middle, with plenty of space for the stamp, the franking and the postman's thumb.

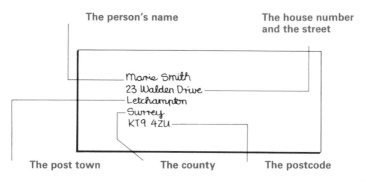

The person's name

The house number and the street

Marie Smith
23 Walden Drive
Letchampton
Surrey
KT9 4ZU

The post town   The county   The postcode

The stages of writing

There are four main stages people usually go through when they write something.

Thinking

What...
1. What to write.
2. What order to do things in.
3. What extra information and ideas you need.

Where...
1. In your head...
If it is not very complicated, you can think as you write.
2. On paper...
If it is a more complicated piece of writing, then you may need to plan things out on paper first.

Research...
Sometimes you may need to find things out before you start writing: from books, or by asking people questions, or by making observations.

Revising

You often find that your writing does not come out quite right first time. You may have to make changes to it. Ask yourself questions like:

1. Is the shape of it right? Are things in the right order?
2. Do all the sentences really mean what I want them to mean?
3. Does it have the impact I want it to?

You can revise your writing in different ways:

1. In your head...
Think your sentences through before you start writing them down.

2. As you write...
Look back over what you have just written and alter it until you are satisfied with it.

3. When you have finished ...
Read what you have written and imagine
that you are someone else reading it.
Change it so that it makes sense to
another reader.

4. Re-writing ...
Sometimes you may find that you need to
rewrite everything.

Writing   Then write your final version.

Checking   When you have finished, you need to
check for mistakes in:

1. *Expression* ...
Read your sentences carefully and make
sure that they are grammatically correct
and do not contain errors of expression.
(There is advice about common errors in
Chapter 15.)

2. *Punctuation* ...
Check your punctuation. (There is advice
about punctuation in Chapter 13.)

3. *Spelling* ...
If in doubt, use a dictionary or ask
someone. (There is advice about spelling
in Chapter 12.)

12: Spelling

What is involved?

It is important to remember that spelling is just a way of writing down the words we use in Spoken English so that other people can understand what we are writing. It was only quite recently that English spelling was standardized. For hundreds of years people could and did spell many words in more than one way. Even today there are very few people who are perfect spellers. Most people have to use a dictionary to check words they are not sure about.

Advice about spelling

1. Never avoid using a new word just because you are not sure how to spell it.
2. Get into the habit of using a dictionary to check spellings you are not sure about.
3. If possible keep a personal list of difficult words in a notebook or diary, for reference. (See the list at the end of this chapter.)
4. If you are not sure which of two or three spellings is the right one, try writing the alternatives out on a piece of paper and see which one looks right.
5. Read regularly. Reading will not make everyone a perfect speller, but it is difficult to be a really good speller if you never read anything at all.
6. Playing the games on pages 164, 166, 168, 169 and 170 will sharpen up your spelling.

Common spelling rules

Plural means 'more than one'. Most words follow these rules:

1. Normally, just add s.

   book ⟶ books
   complication ⟶ complications

2. Words that end in —s, add es.

   glass ⟶ glasses
   genius ⟶ geniuses

3. Words that end in —x and —z, add es.

   box ⟶ boxes
   buzz ⟶ buzzes

4. Words that end in —ch and —sh, add es.

   branch ⟶ branches
   bush ⟶ bushes

5. Words that end in —f, or —fe change the ending to —ve and add s.

   calf ⟶ calves
   wife ⟶ wives

   Exceptions: beliefs   chiefs   dwarfs
         griefs   gulfs   proofs   roofs.

6. Words that end in —y:

   a) If the letter before the y is a vowel, just add s.

     day ⟶ days
     boy ⟶ boys

   b) If the letter before the y is a consonant, change the —y to —ies.

     baby ⟶ babies
     spy ⟶ spies

7. Words that end in —o: usually just need an s.

    piano ⟶ pianos.

Exceptions: a few words add es:

    buffaloes
    cargoes
    dominoes
    echoes
    goes
    grottoes
    haloes
    heroes
    mangoes
    mosquitoes
    mottoes
    potatoes
    tomatoes
    tornadoes
    torpedoes
    volcanoes

8. Words that stay the same in the plural:

    aircraft   deer   sheep

9. Words that change in a different way:

    child ⟶ children
    man ⟶ men
    foot ⟶ feet
    goose ⟶ geese
    mouse ⟶ mice
    tooth ⟶ teeth
    woman ⟶ women

10. Latin and Greek words:

    crisis ⟶ crises
    formula ⟶ formulae

Adding suffixes to verbs

When we use verbs we have to change them according to the sentence they are in:

I always walk to school. I walked to school yesterday, and I am walking to school now.

-ing and -ed

1. Normally you just add -ing and -ed. The rules that follow describe the main exceptions.

2. Words with one syllable, with a long vowel, ending in -e. Remove the e and add -ed and -ing:

rake ⟶ raked ⟶ raking
dare ⟶ dared ⟶ daring
But note: age ⟶ aged ⟶ ageing
　　　　queue ⟶ queued ⟶ queueing

3. Words with one syllable, with a short vowel, ending in a single consonant. Double the consonant and add -ed and -ing:

tap ⟶ tapped ⟶ tapping
beg ⟶ begged ⟶ begging

4. Words with more than one syllable, ending in a single consonant.

a) If the stress is on the last syllable, double the consonant:

propel ⟶ propelled ⟶ propelling

b) If the stress is not on the last syllable, just add -ed and -ing:

benefit ⟶ benefited ⟶ benefiting
budget ⟶ budgeted ⟶ budgeting
sharpen ⟶ sharpened ⟶ sharpening

5. Words ending in -l.

a) If there is only a single vowel before the l, add -led and -ling:

compel ⟶ compelled ⟶ compelling

101

b) If there is a double vowel before the l, just add -ed and -ing:

coil ⟶ coiled ⟶ coiling
peel ⟶ peeled ⟶ peeling

6. Words ending in -y.

a) If the letter before the y is a vowel, just add -ed and -ing:

play ⟶ played ⟶ playing

Exceptions: say ⟶ said
pay ⟶ paid
lay ⟶ laid

b) If the letter before the y is a consonant, change the y to an i before -ed.

cry ⟶ cried ⟶ crying

-s You often have to add -s to a verb:

I walk ⟶ she walks

The rules for doing this are the same as the rules for adding -s to make a plural.

Adding suffixes to adjectives

-ly We can turn adjectives into adverbs by adding -ly:

He is a quick worker: he works quickly.

Usually you just add -ly to the adjective, but there are some exceptions.

1. If the word ends -ll, just add -y:
full ⟶ fully

2. If a word of two or more syllables ends in -y, cut off the -y and add -ily:
happy ⟶ happily

3. One syllable words ending in -y are usually regular:
shy ⟶ shyly

Exception: gay becomes gaily, day becomes daily

102

-er and -est We can add -er and -est to adjectives when we want to make comparisons:

He is a quick worker.
She is a quicker worker than him.
I am the quickest worker in the class.

Normally you just add -er or -est to the adjective, but there are exceptions.

1. Words ending in -y: if there is a consonant before the y, change the y to an i:

happy ⟶ happier ⟶ happiest

2. Words with one syllable, with a long vowel, ending in -e. Remove the e and add -er and -est:

late ⟶ later ⟶ latest

3. Words with one syllable, with a short vowel, ending in a single consonant. Double the consonant and add -er and -est:

sad ⟶ sadder ⟶ saddest

4. Words with one syllable ending in -l: normally just add -er, or -est, but there is an exception:

cruel ⟶ crueller ⟶ cruellest

Other rules

-ie- and -ei-

The rule is: 'i before e except after c, when the sound is long ee.'

thief   receive   piece   ceiling

Exceptions: seize   weir   weird

-ce or -se

The rule is 'c for a noun and s for a verb' – easy to remember because the letters are in alphabetical order: C, N(oun), S, V(erb).

noun	verb
advice	advise
practice	practise
licence	license

Example: I need your advice: will you advise me?

-ise, -ize, -yse

Many verbs and some nouns end in -ise or -ize.

1. Verbs can be made by adding -ize to an adjective or a noun:

modern ——▸ modernize
symbol ——▸ symbolize

2. Many common nouns and verbs ending with the 'eyes' sound are spelled -ise:

advertise	devise	prise (open)
advise	disguise	revise
arise	enterprise	supervise
compromise	exercise	surprise
despise	improvise	televise

Notice that these are not words made directly from other words.

3. A very small number of common words end in -ize:

size   prize

4. A small number of words which come from Greek end in -yse:

paralyse   analyse

-er, -ar, -or Certain verbs can be made into nouns by adding -er (or -r if the verb ends in -e):

design ⟶ designer

make ⟶ maker

A number of other words end with the same 'er' sound, but are spelled differently. These just have to be learned. Here are some of the commonest.

-ar		-or
beggar	particular	actor
burglar	peculiar	doctor
calendar	pillar	inspector
circular	popular	sailor
familiar	regular	visitor
liar	vinegar	creator

Also remember

miner = someone who digs underground;
minor = a person under 18.

-ful and -fully You can make certain nouns into other nouns, or into adjectives by adding 'full', but when you do that, it turns into -ful:

hand + full = handful

shame + full = shameful

When you turn an adjective made like this into an adverb, you add -ly:

shameful ⟶ shamefully

105

-able and -ible   These two are easy to get wrong. There is no easy rule to learn, so you will find that you have to learn many of these words individually.

-able   is more common. It is a living suffix, which means that it is still being used to make new words. It is quite a popular one, too:

'Do you think *anyone* can windsurf across the Atlantic?'
'Oh yes: the Atlantic is definitely very windsurfable these days.'

-ible   is a dead suffix, used in words which come from Latin. The commonest of these are:

accessible	digestible	permissible
admissible	divisible	possible
audible	edible	responsible
collapsible	flexible	reversible
combustible	gullible	sensible
comprehensible	incredible	visible
contemptible	indelible	
credible	invisible	
defensible	legible	

106

-ance/-ant and -ence/-ent

1. Words ending in -ant and -ent are usually adjectives.

2. If there is an -ant and an -ent version of a word, the -ant one is a noun and the -ent one is an adjective:

Noun	Adjective
dependant	dependent
pendant	pendent

3. Words ending in -ance and -ence are usually nouns.

4. -ant adjectives go with -ance nouns:
important (adj)   importance (n)

5. -ent adjectives go with -ence nouns:
different (adj)   difference (n)

6. If the letter before is a t or a v, then it is usually -ant/-ance.

Remember . . .
current = a flow of water, air or electricity
currant = dried fruit

A strong currant!

Apart from that, you have really got to learn them.

Words that are easily confused

These words sound the same and are spelled differently, or are in other ways easily confused. If you are not sure about how any of these words are used, they are explained on pages 136–142.

accept	except	past	passed
affect	effect	peace	piece
aloud	allowed	peninsula	peninsular
aught	ought	pier	peer
bail	bale	principle	principal
bear	bare	quite	quiet
birth	berth	rain	reign
board	bored	read	reed
check	cheque	red	read
chord	cord	right	write
chose	choose	ring	wring
calendar	colander	sail	sale
diary	dairy	sell	cell
dinghy	dingy	sew	sow
draft	draught	some	sum
foul	fowl	stationary	stationery
great	grate	steak	stake
hall	haul	tale	tail
heel	heal	there	their they're
here	hear	threw	through
kerb	curb	to	two
lose	loose	wait	weight
made	maid	weak	week
manner	manor	weather	whether wether
meter	metre	where	wear
miner	minor	were	we're
new	knew	which	witch
no	know	whose	who's
pain	pane	wood	would
pair	pear pare	your	you're

Single and double letters

A common spelling problem concerns words with single and/or double letters. Here is a list of the commonest:

accelerate	exaggerate	patrol
accommodation	fulfil	pedal
address	happiness	possess
assist	harass	professional
beginning	illustrate	questionnaire
brilliant	imitate	sheriff
caterpillar	immediate	success
collapse	marvel	sufficient
collect	mattress	terrible
commit	millenium	tranquillity
corridor	millionaire	transmit
disappear	necessary	unnecessary
discuss	occasion	woollen
embarrass	omit	
paraffin	parallel	

Other problems

adaptation (not adaption)	councillor (council member)	hallelujah
adviser		hypocrite
alleluia	counsel (advice)	kilometre
brand-new	counsellor (adviser)	labyrinth
computer	desiccated	literature
conjuror	enclose	miniature
connection	encyclopedia	moustache
conqueror	forty	rhyme
conscience	gauge	rhythm
conscientious	grandad	somersault
conscious	granddaughter	wagon
council (assembly)	guerrilla	yoghurt

13: Punctuation

Why punctuate?

If we do not use punctuation at all, written English looks very strange indeed:

```
whatspunctuationandwhatsitforpunctuation
isasystemofspacesfullstopscapitalletters
commasandothermarksweuseitwhenwewritetos
eparatewordsandsentencesfromeachotheriti
salsoimportantasawayofmakingthemeaningof
sentencesclearspeciallywhentheycontainan
umberofdifferentclausesasthisonedoes
```

Without any punctuation at all, and this includes the spacing between words, writing becomes almost impossible to read. Yet in the past, writers used far less punctuation than we do today.

Today people read far more and are often in a hurry. Punctuation makes it easier for the eye to travel over the page and pick up quickly the pattern of what is being said.

This chapter also contains information and advice on:

Capital letters

Capital letters are used for these purposes:

1. As the first letter of a sentence.

2. For the personal pronoun 'I'.

3. At the beginning of a new piece of direct speech. (See page 120.)

   Jo shouted, 'Look at that balloon in the sky!'

4. For the first letter of proper nouns:
   - people's names: Caroline Mary Branham
   - places: Branham Court, Branham, Borsetshire
   - titles of books, plays, films, TV programmes: *The Nine O'Clock News*
   - days of the week: Tuesday
   - months of the year: November
   - planets and stars: Betelgeuse

5. For the first letters of titles of people and organizations:
   Councillor Williams
   Lord Winston
   Prime Minister
   National Association for the Care and Resettlement of Offenders

6. For initials in people's names:
   A.J.P. Taylor

7. For initial letters used in abbreviations:
   AAA   SRN   ITV

8. To provide emphasis, for example, in advertising and publicity material.

Full stops, question marks, exclamation marks

Normal sentences must end with one of these three marks. Statements normally end with a full stop.

A full stop marks the end of a sentence.

A question normally ends with a question mark.

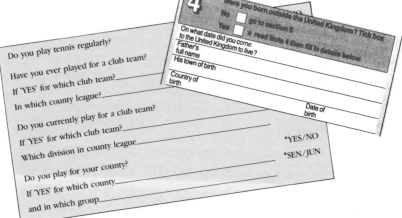

Do you play tennis regularly?

Have you ever played for a club team?

If 'YES' for which club team?_____

In which county league?_____

Do you currently play for a club team?

If 'YES' for which club team?_____

Which division in county league_____

Do you play for your county?

If 'YES' for which county_____

and in which group_____

4 Were you born outside the United Kingdom? Tick box
No ☐ go to section 5
Yes ☐ ✱ read Note 4 then fill in details below.

On what date did you come to the United Kingdom to live?

Father's full name

His town of birth

Country of birth

Date of birth

*YES/NO

*SEN/JUN

Exclamation marks are used to mark an exclamation, or a forceful statement.

Warning: if you use too many exclamation marks, readers will get very tired of them.

Abbreviations

If a word is shortened, or abbreviated, then you usually put a full stop after it.

P.G. Wodehouse
3 kilometres S.(South)
Tenn.(Tennessee)
Sqn.Ldr. (Squadron Leader)

There are a number of exceptions to this:

1. Abbreviations made up only of capital letters do not need full stops:

AAA   IOW   SRN   BBC   UN

2. Abbreviations that make up words (acronyms) do not need full stops:

ASH   (Action on Smoking and Health)
COSIRA   (Council for Small Industries in Rural Areas)

3. These abbreviations do not need full stops:

Mr   Mrs   M (Monsieur)   Mme (Madame)   Mlle (Mademoiselle)   Dr
St   Revd p (= penny or pence)

Commas

Commas are used to help the reader's eye as it passes over the page of print. If we did not use them at all, sentences could become difficult, or even impossible, to understand. Try reading the next paragraph, which has been printed without commas:

Although everybody says that camping is fun I didn't enjoy our holiday under canvas last summer. The trouble began as soon as we started to put up the tent with Dad in charge. Reading from the instruction booklet he started to shout instructions at Jenny a friend who was camping with us and me. Things went all right at first. We opened the bags and emptied out all the contents: the frame the pegs the inner tent the outer tent and the guy ropes. Then we started to put it together. Just as we had got the framework up Dad's voice boomed out to tell us we had got it all wrong!

As you can see, it would be much easier to read if there were some commas in the right places:

1. To separate the items in a list:
We opened the bags and emptied out all the contents: the frame, the pegs, the inner tent, the outer tent, and the guy ropes.

2. To separate the clauses in a sentence:
Although everybody says that camping is fun, I didn't enjoy our holiday under canvas last summer.
Just as we had got the framework up, Dad's voice boomed out to tell us we had got it all wrong!

3. To mark off phrases that are separate from the main part of the sentence:
The trouble began as soon as we started to put up the tent, with Dad in charge.

4. To mark off clauses or phrases as brackets do:
Reading from the instruction booklet, he started to shout instructions at Jenny, a friend who was camping with us, and me.

Commas are more difficult to use well than any other punctuation mark. This is because it is sometimes partly a matter of personal choice whether to use one or not. Learning how to use commas well takes a long time. You will learn more quickly if you enjoy reading and pay attention to how other writers use them. Reading aloud – your own writing and other people's – also helps you to see where commas should go.

Colons and semi-colons

Colons   Colons are used to introduce a list, a saying, or a statement:

You know, I found the most extraordinary collection of things in his jacket pockets: two penknives, some used chewing-gum, a five pound note, half a false moustache, and the key to his father's filing cabinet.

When they were near the top of the mountain, their leader turned and addressed them: 'Listen to me, all of you. What we are going to do now is very dangerous.'

There is only one rule on board this ship: don't rock the boat.

Semi-colons   A semi-colon is used between two clauses in a sentence. It makes a stronger pause in the sentence than a comma, but not as strong as a full stop. It is often used to separate two or more equal parts in a sentence:

Soccer is a game for gentlemen played by ruffians; rugger is a game for ruffians played by gentlemen.

It was a pitiful scene: some huddled together for warmth; some tried desperately to escape; others stood stunned and motionless.

Apostrophes

Apostrophes are used for two purposes:

1. to show possession (that something belongs to somebody).

2. to show omission (that something has been missed out).

Possession

a) Normally you add 's

That is the dog's basket, not the cat's.

That is Max's book.

b) When the word is a plural ending in s, we just add '

That is the girls' tennis ball.

Notice that these words do not have an apostrophe:

hers   ours   yours   theirs   whose

When *its* means 'of it', you should not put an apostrophe.

Omission

When we are writing informally, or writing speech, we often use shortened forms:

he is ⟶ he's
they are ⟶ they're
I do not ⟶ I don't
it is ⟶ it's

In these cases, the apostrophe shows where the letters have been missed out.

Writing down speech

There are three ways in which you can write down what someone says:

1. script
2. direct speech
3. reported speech

Script is normally used for plays.
Direct speech is most commonly used in stories.
Reported speech is used in reports and also in stories.

Script

MAYOR	(Worried) I've just heard there's a flood on its way!
1ST COUNCILLOR	This is a job for Desperate Dan!

(A deep rumbling noise is heard.)

	Dan will build a dam!
2ND COUNCILLOR	... or make a giant pump!
3RD COUNCILLOR	... or dig a huge trench!

(Dan is swept into the room on a surfboard.)

MAYOR	... or take up surfing!

Notes

1. The names of the speakers are put in capital letters, on the left-hand side of the page.

2. The words spoken are written, without any special punctuation, a little way to the right. The speeches should all start at the same point in the line.

3. Information about an individual character who is speaking, is put in the speech. It is put in brackets and underlined. In print, it is usually set in *italics*.

4. Information about other things that happen, including sounds and actions, is given a line to itself. It is put in brackets and underlined (or in *italics* in a printed text).

Direct speech

The Mayor was very worried. 'I've just heard,' he said, 'there's a flood on its way.'

'This is a job for Desperate Dan!' said one of the councillors. 'Dan will build a dam,' he continued.

A deep rumbling noise filled the air. Another councillor said, '... Or make a giant pump!'

Notes

1. Each piece of speech is enclosed by double or single inverted commas. In books single inverted commas are normally used. In school, pupils are often taught to use double inverted commas.

2. Every new piece of speech must begin with a capital letter, even if it is not the first word in the sentence. This is true except where it is broken by 'he' or 'she said' as in the sentence at the top of this page.

3. Each piece of speech must end with a full stop or an exclamation mark or a question mark *before* the concluding inverted commas ...

4. ... unless the sentence is going to continue, when it ends with a comma. This also comes *before* the concluding inverted commas.

5. When a piece of speech comes in the middle of a sentence it must have a comma (or sometimes a colon) just before the opening inverted commas.

6. For each new speaker you start a new line and usually indent.

7. When something happens, or there is a sound or you want to describe how someone felt, you just write it as part of the story.

Reported speech

Sometimes we want to *report* on what has been said. For example, in a newspaper or magazine article, or when we are telling a story very briefly. This is how the same conversation would appear in full reported speech.

The Mayor was very worried. He said that he had just heard that there was a flood on its way. One of the councillors suggested that it was a job for Desperate Dan: he would build a dam. A deep rumbling noise filled the air. Another councillor said that Dan might make a giant pump.

Differences

The main differences between reported and direct speech are that in reported speech:

1. The words spoken are introduced by *that*.

2. Usually the verb changes:
   is becomes *was*
   have becomes *had*
   was becomes *had been*
   will be becomes *would be*
   and so on.

3. Inverted commas are not used.

It is also possible to write a brief report of a conversation, in which just the main lines of the conversation are reported:

The mayor discussed the approaching floods with the Council. Their discussions were interrupted by a deep rumbling noise.

14: Grammar

Sentences

There are four main types of sentence.

Statement This is a statement.

Question What is the question?

Command Give me a command.

Exclamation What a strange exclamation that was!

Sentences and clauses A sentence can be made up of one or more clauses:

I play football
[CLAUSE]

I play football   but my brother plays marbles.
[CLAUSE]   +   [CLAUSE]

I don't understand   what you are talking about.
[CLAUSE]   +   [CLAUSE]

Parts of a clause

Verb A clause must normally contain a complete verb.

I *play* football.

play is a complete verb; *playing* is not complete – it is not therefore a complete clause, to say:

'I playing on the grass.'

In this case the complete verb is *am playing*:

'I am playing on the grass.'

Subject	Statements, questions and exclamations normally contain a subject. In statements it usually comes at the beginning and tells us what the clause is going to be about.

I play football.

In questions it may come before or after the verb, or even in the middle of it, depending on the kind of question:

Who is that over there?
Are *you* afraid?
Are *you* coming with us?

Object	The object normally comes after the verb in statements. The object is the person or thing that is affected by the action of the verb.

The dog bit *the postman*.
I love *fast cars*.

In questions the object also comes after the verb:

Do you like *ice-cream*?

unless it is a *question word*:

What are you doing?

Complement	The complement is a part of the clause that provides more information about another part. It often comes after verbs like *to be*, *to seem*, *to appear*, *to become*. In these sentences it tells us more about the subject:

You seem *very happy*.
He has just become a *father*.

In other sentences it tells us more about the object, which it follows:

[SUBJECT] [OBJECT] [COMPLEMENT]
The news made Sandra *very sad*.

Adverb Adverbs generally answer the questions: *when? where? why? how?*

I met him *later*	at nine o'clock
I met him *nearby*	outside the cinema
I met him *intentionally*	for a very good reason
I met him *accidentally*	by chance

They can appear in different places in the clause:

Suddenly I met your friend.
I saw *suddenly* the look on his face.
We met *suddenly*.

Compound sentences You can join clauses together just by using words like *and* or *but*:

I play netball. + My sister likes tennis. + My brother does not play games.

I play netball *and* my sister likes tennis *but* my brother does not play games.

In compound sentences, all the clauses are grammatically equal. It is fairly simple to divide these sentences up into simple sentences:

I was walking through the shopping centre [and] I caught sight of Granny [but] it was very crowded [and] I lost her again.

I was walking through the shopping centre.
I caught sight of Granny.
It was very crowded.
I lost her again.

Complex sentences

In complex sentences the clauses are joined together in a different way. Suppose you want to join these two clauses together:

Mum was cross.
I did not meet Granny.

If you make a compound sentence using *and*, you have not got a lot of choice:

Mum was cross and I did not meet Granny.
I did not meet Granny and Mum was cross.

Either way it does not tell you why or when things happened. A complex sentence does. A complex sentence has a *main* clause, which usually tells you the main thing in the sentence, and *subordinate* clauses which are related to it in some way.

Mum was cross *because*	I did not meet Granny.
[MAIN]	[SUBORDINATE]

Because Mum was cross	I did not meet Granny.
[SUBORDINATE]	[MAIN]

You can link the two clauses in lots of other ways too:

Mum was cross so I didn't meet Granny.
Although Mum was cross I didn't meet Granny.
While Mum was cross I didn't meet Granny.
Each sentence has a different meaning.

Phrases

A phrase is a single word, or a linked group of words, that forms part of a clause.

Noun phrase A noun phrase can form the subject or the object of a sentence:

David is my brother.
He likes *vanilla ice-cream with plenty of chocolate sauce on it.*

The complement of a sentence can also be a noun phrase:

They made her *the captain of the team.*

Verb phrase This may just be one word:

He *likes* sweets.

Some verb phrases can be very long:

I *should have been able to guess* her name.
You *were supposed to be trying to win.*

Adverb phrase An adverb phrase can be one or more adverbs:

She ran *quickly*.
He ran *really rather slowly*.

Many adverb phrases contain no adverbs. They just work as an adverb in the sentence.

I met her *on the steps of St Paul's Cathedral.*

Adjective phrase The complement of a sentence can be an adjective phrase. This may be based on one or more adjectives.

He was *tall*.
He was *very tall, dark, and handsome.*

It may also contain other words:

He was very tall, dark, and handsome, *with piercing blue eyes.*

Word classes

Words can be divided into word classes according to the way in which they are used in sentences. Many words can be used in more than one way, and so belong to more than one class. It is useful to know what word class, or classes, a word belongs to for several reasons:

1. When you look a word up in a dictionary, you will see what class(es) it belongs to and so learn how it is used in sentences.

2. It is difficult to talk about writing unless you have the right words to use. The names for word classes are some of the words you need.

3. Learning about how words work in sentences can be very useful to you as a reader, when you are trying to understand long and complicated sentences.

There are eight main word classes in English:

Nouns	Prepositions
Adjectives	Conjunctions
Verbs	Pronouns
Adverbs	Articles

127

Verbs

Definition

A verb is a word, or number of words, which shows what a person or thing is doing. Verbs are at the centre of any sentence: they are usually in the middle, after the subject and before the object or complement, if there is one. They are also at the centre, because it is difficult to write a sentence that makes sense without a verb.

Most verbs will fit into one of these three spaces:

1. He _____ it.

2. She _____.

3. It _____ good.

Some verbs will fit more than one of the spaces:

is playing (1. & 2.)
appeared (2. & 3.)

Examples of these three are:

1. *likes*   2. *runs*   3. *is*

Types of verb We can divide verbs into three groups according to the way in which they are used in a sentence:

1. Transitives These are verbs that can be followed by an object:

break: I have broken an egg.

2. Intransitives These are verbs that do not have to be followed by an object:

swim: I have been swimming.

Some verbs can be used either transitively or intransitively:

She is playing tennis.
She is playing.

3. Linking These are verbs that are followed by a complement:

seem: Mary seems very pleased with herself.

Forms of a verb Most verbs have these forms:

base: miss, ring
infinitive: to miss, to ring
present participle: missing, ringing
past form: missed, rang
past participle: missed, rung

Auxiliary verbs There are other forms of the verb, which
we make by using a group of special verbs
called *auxiliaries*:
Primary: is, was, etc;   have, had, etc;
do, did, etc.
Primary auxiliaries tell us about things
that actually happen. (I *have been*
walking.)
Modal: may, might, can, could, shall,
should, will, would, must.
Modal auxiliaries tell us about things
that might happen. (I *could* walk.)

Past, present,
future We change the form of the verb, and
combine it with auxiliaries, to show:

when something happened;
how something happened;
our *thoughts* and *feelings* about what
happened.

129

Nouns

Nouns are words that refer to people, places, things and ideas:

cake thought child sand butter homework Tuesday John

When they are used in sentences, nouns are words that will fit into one of these gaps:

That is a _____.
I have got some _____.
This is _____.

Types of noun	Nouns can be divided into different groups:
1. Countable:	Things that can be counted and so have a plural (usually ending in ——s). Words like: biscuit, thought, child.
or **Uncountable:**	Things that cannot be counted and normally have no plural. Words like: sand, butter, homework.
2. Concrete:	Things you can touch, taste, feel, see, or smell. Words like: biscuits, butter, sand.
or Abstract:	Thoughts, ideas, and things that cannot be touched, tasted, etc. Words like: thought, speed, beauty.
3. Proper:	Names of particular people, places, months, days. Words like: John, London, September, Tuesday.
4. Common:	All the other nouns.

Adjectives

Definition

Adjectives work with nouns. They help to make the meaning of
the noun clearer or fuller.

Most adjectives will fit into one or more of
these five groups:

1. Words that can be used with a noun in
   this way:

   a _____ [noun]
   an _____ [noun]
   the _____ [noun]
   For example: an empty teapot.

2. Words that can be used as a
   complement, like this:
   The [noun] is _____.
   For example: the book is exciting.

3. Words that can be modified by very:
   a very difficult problem

4. Words that can be used in
   comparisons:
   _____er   _____est
   or more _____   most _____
   happier   happiest
   more unusual   most unusual

5. Words that can be turned into adverbs
   by adding —ly:
   happy ——→happily

I'm a happy, blissful,
ecstatic, elated, joyous,
merry adjective.

Adverbs

This is a very large and mixed class of words.

Definition

1. Adverbs work with verbs. They help to make the meaning of the verb clearer or fuller.

2. Adverbs work with adjectives. They can make them weaker or stronger or more emphatic.

3. Adverbs work with other adverbs. They can make them weaker or stronger or more emphatic.

Adverbs and Verbs

When an adverb works with a verb it usually answers one of these questions:

How? – He ran quickly towards the station.

When? – We visited Grandma yesterday.

Where? – We saw Peter there.

Adverbs and Adjectives

Examples:
The Pekinese was ugly.
How ugly?
Astoundingly ugly.

Adverbs with other Adverbs

Examples:
The car was travelling fast.
How fast?
It was going really very fast indeed.

Prepositions

Definition

Prepositions are the 'little words' of English – words like in, out, up, down, by, for. As their name suggests, they are *positioned* before (*pre*) other words: a noun or noun phrase, or certain adverbs:

up the stairs

under the dog

in the pond

through the cat-flap

This is a list of some of the commonest single word prepositions in English:

about	down	round
above	during	since
across	for	through
among	from	throughout
around	in	till
at	into	to
before	near	under
behind	off	underneath
below	on	until
beneath	onto	up
between	opposite	with
beyond	over	without
by	past	

Pronouns

**Personal
pronouns**

Personal pronouns can be the subject or
the object of a sentence:

Subject	Object
I	me
you	you
we	us
he	him
she	her
they	them
it	it

We have lost *them.*

Reflexive pronouns: these refer back. This
means that they refer back to the subject
of the sentence:

She has hurt *herself.*

Some possessive pronouns are used with a
noun:

my   your   his   her   our   their   its

That's *my* ball!

Others stand on their own in a sentence:

mine   yours   his   hers   ours   theirs

Is this ball *yours*?

**Relative
pronouns**

who   whom   whose   that   which
These are used to introduce relative
(adjective) clauses:

This is the house *that* Jack built.

**Interrogative
pronouns**

who   whom   whose   what   which
These are used to ask questions:

What is that funny thing on the end of
your nose?

Demonstrative pronouns	this that these those

Demonstrative pronouns

this   that   these   those

These point things out:

This is the book I want, not that.

Odds and ends

There are also a number of other words that can be used as pronouns:

all	each	one
another	enough	other
any	every	several
anybody	half	some
anyone	no one	somebody
anything	nobody	someone
both	nothing	something

Conjunctions

Conjunctions are words that join other words together. In particular they join phrases and clauses. They are words like:

and   but   nor   or
after   as   before   since   until
when   whenever   while
where   wherever
how   however
as   because   since
although   if   unless

Articles

This is the smallest word class. It contains three words:

a   an   the

15: Getting it right

Problems ... problems

This chapter describes some of the commonest problems people have when writing English:

**problems with words,
problems with sentences,
problems with punctuating,
paragraphing.**

Where there is an asterisk * before something, it means that it is not good English.

Problems with words

a bit

Not *abit. There are a number of phrases like this, which people try to turn into single words: a lot, in front, thank you, and all right.

accept/except

Accept means 'receive from someone'. Except means 'all but'.

affect/effect

Affect is usually a verb: 'The plants have been badly affected by the frost.'
Effect is usually a noun: 'The main effect was that all their leaves dropped off.'

already/all ready

Example: 'Are you all ready? I'm getting bored already, just waiting for you!'

all right

All right is Standard English; *alright is not.

altogether/all together

Altogether is normally an adverb, and is used in sentences like: 'This is an altogether different matter.'
It should not be confused with all (adjective) together (adverb), as in: 'They were playing all together.'

along/a long

Along is an adverb or a preposition: 'They were walking along the street.' 'Run along now, dear.'
A long is part of a noun phrase: 'They have known each other for a long time.'

a lot	Not *alot
aloud/allowed	Aloud is the opposite of silently. Allowed means permitted.
anyone/any one	Anyone means anybody. You use any one when you mean one out of a number: 'There were hundreds of people there and any one of them could have been the criminal.'
anyway/any way	'Anyway, I think they did it.' 'They did it in any way they could.'
aught/ought	Aught means anything. Ought means should.
bail/bale	Bail means empty out. Bale means bundle.
bare/bear	Bare means naked. Bear means carry, or a large animal.
berth/birth	Berth is where a ship is tied up. Birth is when someone is born.
board/bored	Board: as in 'bread board'. Bored: as in 'I'm bored'.
calendar/colander	A calendar is for dates. A colander is for peas.
cell	See sell.
check/cheque	Check means make sure of. A cheque is something you cash.
chord/cord	Chord is a word from geometry and music. A cord is like string.
choose/chose	You should distinguish between: chose as in, 'I chose it yesterday', and choose, as in, 'I shall choose some new clothes'.
continual/ continuous	Continual is used about things that happen again and again: 'I can't stand these continual interruptions!' Continuous is used to describe things that are *not* interrupted: 'She holds the world record for continuous saxophone playing.'
councillor/ counsellor	A councillor is a member of a council. A counsellor is an adviser.
curb/kerb	To curb is to restrain. The kerb is the pavement edge.

dinghy/dingy	A dinghy is a small boat. Dingy means grimy.
draft/draught	A draft is a drawing or version of something. A draught is a current of air. To draft something is to draw it up.
everyone/every one	Everyone means everybody. Every one is used when talking about each individual out of a number: 'There were five hundred people in the audience and every one of them enjoyed the concert.'
flammable/inflammable	The problem is that both flammable and inflammable are correctly used to describe something that can catch fire. So if you think, 'Inflammable must be the opposite of flammable' you will be dangerously wrong. The safest way is to use: flammable = may catch fire non-flammable = will not catch fire
foul/fowl	A foul is an offence at football and other sports. Foul is also an adjective meaning unpleasant. A fowl is a bird, such as a chicken.
gaol/jail	Both are correct, and both are pronounced in the same way.
guard/guide	These two words are sometimes confused. To guard is to protect, and a guard is someone or something who protects. To guide is to show the way, and a guide is someone or something that does so.
hall/haul	The hall is part of a house or other building. To haul is to pull.
have	See of.
heal/heel	To heal means to make or get better. The heel is part of the foot.
hear/here	'I can hear you.' 'I am here.'
I/me	These are sometimes confused, particularly in speech. I is used as a subject, and me is used as an object. So it is, 'My brother and I went to see them'; *not* *'Me and my brother

	went to see them.' Me is used after prepositions: 'Give it to me.' 'Between you and me'; *not* *'Between you and I.'
in front	Not *infront.
jail	See gaol.
kerb	See curb.
lay/lie	These are often confused. The verb lay (past form = laid) is a transitive verb. This means that it should be followed by an object: 'The hen has just laid an egg.' 'You must lay down your weapons.') The verb lie is an intransitive verb, which means that it does not have an object. Its past forms are lay, and lain: 'She likes to lie on her bed. She lay down at five o'clock and she has lain there ever since.'
lightening/ lightning	'This story is rather heavy; it needs lightening.' 'Yesterday I was nearly struck by lightning.'
loose/lose	Loose is the opposite of tight. Lose is the opposite of win.
made/maid	Made is the past form of make. A maid is a girl, or a female servant.
manner/manor	Manner means way. Manor means estate, or house.
meter/metre	A meter is something you measure with. A metre is a distance.
miner/minor	A miner is someone who digs underground. Minor is an adjective meaning lesser, or a noun meaning a young person.
of/have	Have is often shortened to 've, when we speak. This sounds a bit like of. The two should not be confused. Of can never be used with a verb. It is *never* correct to write *could of, or *must of.
ought	See aught.
pain/pane	Pain is physical discomfort. A pane is part of a window.

pair/pear/pare	A pair is two. A pear is a fruit. To pare is to take the rind off.
passed/past	Passed is a verb, the past form of pass: 'I passed her in the street yesterday.' Past can be a noun or an adjective meaning the opposite of future: 'In the past things were different.' Past can also be a preposition: 'We walked past her yesterday.'
peace/piece	Peace is the opposite of war. Piece means a part, or section.
peninsula/ peninsular	Peninsula is a noun. Peninsular is an adjective.
peer/pier	A peer is someone whom you might meet in the House of Lords. You might go on the pier at the seaside.
practicable/ practical	If something is practicable it could be done. If something is practical it is useful or useable.
principal/principle	Principal can be an adjective, meaning main, or a noun, meaning the main or chief person in an organization like a college. Principle is always a noun and means a rule or standard by which people run their lives.
proposal/ proposition	A proposal is a plan which is put forward. A proposition is something which someone puts forward for thinking or talking about.
quiet/quite	Quiet is the opposite of noisy. Quite means almost.
rain/reign	Rain is wet. The Queen reigns.
read/red	Read is a verb. Its past form is read: 'I have read the newspaper today.' This past form is pronounced in the same way as the colour red.
read/reed	You read a book. You might find a reed in a pond, or a clarinet.
right/write	Right means correct, opposite to left. Write means put words on paper.

ring/wring	Ring is what a bell does. Wring is what you do to wet clothes.
sail/sale	You would find a sail in a boat. There might be a sale in a shop.
sell/cell	To sell is to offer something to someone for money. A cell is a small room in a prison.
sew/sow	You sew with a needle and thread. You sow seeds in the ground.
stationary/ stationery	Stationary means not moving. Stationery means envelopes, paper, etc.
stake/steak	A stake is a piece of wood. A steak is a piece of meat.
tale/tail	A tale is a story. A tail is what dogs wag.
thank you	Not *thankyou.
their/there/they're	These three are often confused, especially when writers are in a hurry: their = belonging to them there = opposite to here they're = they are
threw/through	Threw is the past form of throw. Through is a preposition, as in, 'We walked through the park.'
to/too/two	These are often confused by people in a hurry. 'I want to buy two shirts; Mary wants two too.'
wait/weight	You wait for something. Weight means heaviness.
warden/warder	A warden is someone who is in charge of something, for example, a Youth Hostel warden. A warder is someone who is in charge of prisoners in a gaol.
weak/week	Weak means feeble. A week is seven days.
weather/whether/ wether	Weather is rain, sun, etc. Whether is used in sentences like, 'I don't know whether to go or not.' A wether is a sheep.
wear/where	'Where did you put the clothes you are going to wear tomorrow?'

were/we're	These two are sometimes confused. Were is the past form of are. We're is a shortened form of we are.
which/witch	'Which way did you say the witch went on her broomstick?'
who's/whose	Who's = who is Whose = of whom
—wise	Adding —wise to a noun is a way of constructing an adverb (e.g. clockwise). It can be overdone; He may have been a genius education-wise, but he was a total disaster family-wise. This is just a sloppy and wordy way of saying: He may have been good at school, but he was impossible to live with.
wood/would	Wood is made from trees. Would is used in sentences like, 'I would if I could.'
wring	see ring
write	see right
your/you're	Your = belonging to you You're = you are

Sentences

Getting the verb right A lot of sentences go wrong, because the writer fails to get the verb right. Verbs *inflect*: you have to change the form of verbs according to the way in which you wish to use them in the sentence. They change according to *number* and *tense*.

Tense A problem some writers find is changing the *time* of the action from present to past:

It is very dark. We walk slowly through the unlit church. Suddenly we *saw* a strange shape.

or from past to present:

I shrank back in horror: was this the ghost we had all heard so much about? I *decide* to be brave.

The first version of this confusion (starting in the present and then moving to the past) happens much more often than the second. One way of avoiding the problem is to tell stories using past tenses, rather than present tenses, unless there are very good reasons for using the present.

Number A common error is to put a singular verb with a plural subject:

During the concert Dave, my best friend, and my sister, Sandra, *was* sitting very close to the stage.

The subject is made up of two people: *Dave* and *Sandra*, so the verb should be *were sitting*. Ask yourself: 'If I replace the subject words with a pronoun, which pronoun would I use?'

Here the answer would be 'they', so the verb must be plural.

each, every, everyone, and no one

These are all singular: they all refer to *one* of something. They all need the singular form of the verb:

Each of the children *has* been given a present.

none

This can be singular or plural. Both these sentences are correct:

None of the children *is* playing tomorrow.
None of the children *are* playing tomorrow.

his or her/their

Another problem can come up when you use words like *everyone*. What word do you put in this gap?

Everyone has _____ own opinion.

In the past people used to say that the correct word was *his*. Nowadays many people think that this is sexist. Some people solve it by writing *his or her*. This can be very awkward. Many people write *their*. In very formal English this is not acceptable (because *their* is plural) but it is very often used.

Advice: Use *their* unless you are writing for someone who is very strict about these things. Then write *his or her*, or change the sentence round to avoid the problem.

less/fewer, amount/number

Some things you can count, like trees; other things you cannot count, like milk. Nouns can be divided into countable and uncountable. (Some, like *cheese*, can be both.) The rule is:

Use *less* and *amount* with uncountables. (*less milk, a small amount of milk*)

Use *fewer* and *number* with countables. (*fewer coins, a large number of coins*)

Uncountables take a singular verb. Countables (when there are more than one of them) take a plural verb.

Getting things in the right order

*'Wanted: bath for baby with non-slip bottom.'

Parts of a sentence that refer to the same thing should be kept together if possible. The parts of the sentence are linked like this:

wanted	bath
for baby	with non-slip
(= baby's)	bottom

So a better wording is:

'Wanted: baby's bath with non-slip bottom.'

I saw the British Museum riding on the top of a Number 9 bus.

Starting a sentence with -ing

*Coming under the door I felt a draught.

This type of mistake happens because people do not remember that an -ing at the beginning of a clause *must* refer to the subject of that clause. So in this case *coming* must refer to *I*. The correct version is:

I felt a draught coming under the door.

There are particular problems with sentences that start with *being*:

*Being a small school, you can get to know people easily.

Here *being* refers to *you* – which is nonsense. It is impossible to correct the sentence just by turning it round, so you have to rewrite it:

As it is a small school, you can get to know people easily.

Advice: beware of sentences that start with being.

Adverbs

*The lawn needs mowing badly.

You can face problems if you are careless about where you put adverbs. If there is a choice, place the adverb as near as possible to the word or phrase it modifies. In this sentence, the adverb should be modifying *needs*, so the correct word order is:

The lawn badly needs mowing.

Certain adverbs are very useful and can come in many different positions:

Only John wants to see the Eiffel Tower.
John only wants to see the Eiffel Tower.
John wants only to see the Eiffel Tower.
John wants to see only the Eiffel Tower.

Each sentence means something different. When you are speaking you can make your meaning clear by stress and intonation. When you are writing you have to rely on where you place the adverb.

Split infinitives

The infinitive is the 'to-' form of the verb. If you put something between the to and the verb base, you are splitting the infinitive, as in 'to boldly walk'. Some people say you should never split an infinitive. It is true that it can be rather clumsy, but on the other hand there are times when it is perfectly all right. You have to use your common sense.

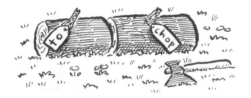

Prepositions at the end of a sentence

Some people say that you should never end a sentence with a preposition, because prepositions are supposed to come before nouns.

This is not a very helpful rule as is shown by the nonsense example:

This is something up with which I will not put.

Most people would prefer:

This is something I will not put up with.

Relative clauses Relative clauses are clauses that work like adjectives in the sentence as a whole:

That is the teacher who used to teach us last year.

They are introduced by relative pronouns:

who   whom   whose   which   that

who/whom In very formal written English *who* is used for the subject of the clause, as in the example above. *Whom* is used as the object, or after a preposition:

That is the teacher whom I met yesterday.
That is the driver by whom I was given a lift.
Whom is used less and less, even in books, and it may eventually disappear.

whose/who's *Whose* means belonging to whom:

Jane is the girl whose coat I borrowed.

Who's is short for *who is*:

Jane is the girl who's coming with us.

Prepositions Sentences with relative clauses in them can get a little complicated. Try not to lose control of what is going on in your sentence, especially when you are using a preposition with a relative pronoun:

*This is the book about which I told you about.

This can be corrected to either of these:

This is the book about which I told you.
This is the book I told you about.

Other sentence problems

... as ... as ...

These two like to go together. If you use *as* to make a comparison, then you must follow it with another *as* to complete the comparison: I am as tall as you.

You should not write, for example:
I am as tall or taller than you.

It should be:
I am as tall as or taller than you.

either ... or
neither ... nor
both ... and not
only ... but also

Sentences that contain these pairs of words can cause problems. It is important to remember that if you use them in a sentence, that sentence has two parallel parts. Each of the two should balance the other:

You are either a bad liar ...
    ... or a very foolish person.

To make sure that you have constructed the sentence correctly, cover up the two words (either ... or, etc.) and everything in between them. What is left should still be a correct sentence:

You are [either a bad liar or] a very foolish person.

If you use a preposition outside the 'either ... or' words, then you do not need to repeat it:

I gave presents to both Julia and Michael.

If you use it inside, then it has to be repeated:

I gave presents both to Julia and to Michael.

Both ... and

Both can only refer to two individuals or groups. You should not write:

I met both James and Julia and Peter in town.

Double negatives

Most people believe that two negatives in a sentence cancel each other out. You may do this deliberately:

I am not unhappy about this. (Meaning that I am quite happy about it.)

If you do not mean it to work like this then it is not Standard English:

*I didn't do nothing.

Many people would disapprove of this, although, in fact, some of our greatest writers, including Shakespeare and Milton, used double negatives in exactly this way: to emphasize their meaning.

Punctuation

Apostrophe

More people seem to find problems with this punctuation mark than with any other. Often this is because they panic: as soon as they see an *s* on the end of a word they reach for the apostrophe. In fact apostrophes are only used with an *s* to show two things:

a) possession (John's car ...)
b) omission (John's gone ...)

The full rule explaining this is on page 109. The best advice to those who still find it difficult is 'If in doubt, leave it out'. You are more likely to be right than wrong if you follow this advice.

Direct speech

This causes trouble sometimes. There are two areas of difficulty.

1. Starting each piece of speech on a new line. This is to make it clear to the reader when a new speaker begins to speak, especially if you are not using words for *she said/he said* every time someone speaks.

2. The punctuation mark that comes before each pair of inverted commas:

John said, '_____.'
'_____,' she replied.

Mistakes are caused in two ways. Often this punctuation mark is simply missed out. Sometimes people place it on the wrong side of the inverted commas. The full rules for this are on page 112.

You cannot use a comma to join two clauses:

John got to the bus-stop + the bus had already gone.

This cannot be joined just with a comma:

*John got to the bus-stop, the bus had already gone.

You must either use a conjunction:

John got to the bus-stop, but the bus had already gone.
When John got to the bus-stop, the bus had already gone.

or a semi-colon:

John got to the bus-stop; the bus had already gone.

Paragraphing

Paragraphing has two main purposes:

1. To help the writer organize his or her writing in a sensible and logical way.

2. To help readers find their way through the piece of writing.

Organizing your writing

When you are planning a piece of writing, especially if it is non-fiction, you will probably find that the subject divides into a number of topics. Sometimes these may break down into smaller sections. Each of these topics and sections can give you material for one or more paragraphs. You should try to make sure that when you move from one topic to another, you start a new paragraph.

Thinking of the reader

Each new paragraph should be separated from the one before. You can do this by indenting: starting the first sentence of the paragraph about 1–2 cm from the beginning of the line.

You should also try to make it clear to the reader that you are starting a new topic and give him or her some idea of what that topic is. This is usually done in the first one or two sentences in the paragraph.

Reading

Paragraphing is not easy at first. You will become a better writer if you keep your eyes and mind open when you read: 'How does the writer of *this* book divide the material up into paragraphs? How does s/he make the move from one paragraph to another clear and easy to understand?'

Part D: Word play

16: Playing with words

Riddles

Nobody knows when human beings first started playing with words: asking riddles, making puns and telling jokes. It was certainly a very long time ago. One of the oldest and most famous riddles is the Riddle of the Sphinx, which dates from the time of the ancient Greeks.

Oedipus and the Sphinx

The Sphinx was a strange creature with the head of a woman, the body of a lion, the tail of a serpent and the wings of an eagle. She had been terrorizing the people of Thebes. She had made her home near the city and stopped travellers going to and from Thebes. She asked them a riddle. If they could not answer it she strangled them and ate them. For quite some time no one was able to solve this riddle.

What creature sometimes has two feet, sometimes three feet and sometimes four feet, and is at its weakest when it has most?

A young man called Oedipus was travelling to Thebes and was stopped by the Sphinx, who asked him the riddle. Oedipus solved it at once: 'The answer is a human being. Humans begin as babies, who crawl on all fours. That is when they are weakest. Then they grow to maturity and walk on two legs. Finally, as they become old they have to walk with a stick, so they have three legs.'

The Sphinx was so angry that it hurled itself over a nearby cliff and was killed.

There are other famous occasions when heroes have had to answer riddles in order to save their lives. In *The Hobbit* by J.R.R. Tolkien, Bilbo Baggins is lost underground and meets an unpleasant, slimy, dangerous creature called Gollum. In order to save his life Bilbo agrees with Gollum that they have a riddle competition. Gollum says that if Bilbo wins, he will show him how to get out of the underground maze. The riddles in this story are based on Anglo-Saxon riddles. These are two of them:

> *A box without hinges, key, or lid.*
> *Yet golden treasure inside is hid.*

> *This thing all things devours:*
> *Birds, beasts, trees, flowers;*
> *Gnaws iron, bites steel;*
> *Grinds hard stones to meal;*
> *Slays king, ruins town,*
> *And beats high mountain down.*

I am the shame beneath a carpet

I am the shame beneath a carpet.
No-one comes to sweep me off my feet.

Abandoned rooms and unread books collect me.
Sometimes I dance like particles of light.

My legions thicken on each window pane,
A gathering of dust, perpetual gloom,

And when at last the house has fallen,
I am the cloud left hanging in the air.

(Answers on page 172.)

Puns

If for every pun I shed
I were to be punished
I would hide my punnish head
Deep inside a puny shed.

A pun is a joke or saying that depends on one word having at least two meanings.

How puns work

In English many words have a number of different meanings. For example:

run: to move fast on foot: 'I want to *run* away.'
run: to organize things: 'I want to *run* the football team.'
run: to continue: 'The show has been running for some time.'

Puns also use *homophones*: words that are spelled differently, but sound the same. For example:

write   right   wright   rite

They can take this even further, combining words to make a more complicated pun:

My sister's gone to the Caribbean.
Jamaica?
No. She wanted to go.

'Knock, Knock' jokes

'Knock, Knock' jokes are based on puns, but they often use names as well as common nouns:

Others are more complicated:

Knock, knock.
Who's there?
Cornflakes.
Cornflakes who?
I'll tell you next week. It's a cereal.

Knock, knock.
Who's there?
Cows go.
Cows go who?
No – cows go moo!

Crazy definitions

People who like puns also enjoy making up or solving crazy definitions. Giles Brandreth is an enthusiast for this kind of thing. Here are some of his:

cartoon	song that cars sing
crowbar	where birds go for a drink
half-wit	someone who is funny half the time
hatchet	what a hen does with an egg
myth	an unmarried moth
pillow	headquarters
robin	a bird that steals

Quiz

What words are these the crazy definitions for?
(Answers on page 172.)

a sick bird of prey
what you kiss with
what a mother does with a baby to get it to sleep
when your clothes wear out
glum drops

The rebus

Another puzzle or game that involves guessing words or phrases is the rebus. The name comes from a Latin word meaning 'by things'. This is because it consists of defining words by means of things: letters, numbers, pictures and little diagrams.

Examples   One of the best known rebuses is:

Too wise you are;
Too wise you be.
I see you are
Too wise for me.

Other rebuses use pictures as well as letters and numbers to spell out a message.

Quiz

What do these rebuses mean? (Answers on page 172.)

1 arrest	2 one the other	3 C SP H	4 STAND
you're	one the other		I
	one the other		
	one the other		
	one the other		
	one the other		

Word squares

A word square is an arrangement of words in which the letters make words in both directions: across from left to right, and down. Usually the across words and the down words are the same:

```
H A T
A P E
T E A
```

They are fun to make up and, roughly speaking, the shorter the words, the easier it is to make a square. So a five-letter square is fairly easy, but a seven-letter square is very difficult:

```
N E S T L E S
E N T R A N T
S T R A N G E
T R A I T O R
L A N T E R N
E N G O R G E
S T E R N E R
```

Crosswords

Crosswords are well known to most people: they are to be found in newspapers, magazines, and books.

The basic crossword is very simple. A grid of squares is provided with some of the squares blacked out. You are given *clues* to the words that are required to fill in the squares. There are different types of clue.

Straightforward

Usually some kind of definition:

The game of squares you are playing now (9): CROSSWORD

General knowledge

It is the highest mountain in the world (5, 7): MOUNT EVEREST

Anagram

Orc Swords (anag.) (9): CROSSWORD

Hidden anagram

Letter-puzzle that confuses Ross crowd (9): CROSSWORD

Here the word *confuses* gives you a clue that the letters of the word have been confused – jumbled up to form an anagram.

Hidden word

A word puzzle in mi*cros? Sword* play will reveal it (9): CROSSWORD

Cryptic

Never one of these if you want to solve it (9): CROSSWORD

Clues like this are usually in two parts. One part gives some kind of definition of the word: . . . *if you want to solve it.* The other part gives a more hidden clue. It refers to the saying, 'Never a cross word . . .'

Anagrams

An anagram mixes the letters of a word in such a way as to make another word or words.

If possible the new word should be something that fits the meaning of the old word. For example one anagram of angered is enraged. Anagrams are made of single words, names, and phrases.

Single words

is no amity animosity
moon-starers astronomers
tender names endearments
excitation intoxicate
ideals ladies
a grim era marriage
carthorse orchestra
court poser prosecutor
a stew sir? waitress

Now you try

Can you work out what each of these is an anagram for? (Answers on page 172.)

voices rant on
unclear
on tip
nine thumps
is no meal
it ran

These are the names of four famous people, past and present. (Answers on page 172.)

Old West Action
That Great Charmer
I may rue the show
We all make his praise

Palindromes

These are words or phrases that read the same in both directions.

They include words like deed, names like Anna, and even whole sentences like Nurse, I spy gypsies, run! Here are a few more:

God! a dog!
Draw, O coward!
Niagara, O roar again!
Sad? I'm Midas.
Dennis and Edna sinned.
Snug & raw was I ere I saw war & guns.
Live not on evil.
Adam, I'm Ada.
'Tis Ivan on a visit.
No, it is opposition.

Spoonerisms

Spoonerisms are named after The Revd William Spooner, who was Warden of New College, Oxford, at the beginning of this century. He had the unfortunate habit of accidentally swapping the first letters or even syllables of words. For example, he is supposed to have said that cyclists need well-boiled icicles. Here are some other famous Spoonerisms:

I have in my bosom a half-warmed fish.

A blushing crow.

The Lord is a shoving leopard.

In church: Please sew me to another sheet; someone is occupewing my pie.

You were fighting a liar in the quadrangle.

You have hissed my mystery lectures; you have tasted a whole worm. You will leave Oxford on the next town drain.

Acrostics

An acrostic is a piece of writing, usually a poem, in which each line begins with a letter from a key word. As a result you can read the word downwards on the left-hand side of the page. Some acrostics have words at the beginning and end of the lines.

Having this
One can
Please oneself in
Everything.

A much more complicated and poetic acrostic was written by Lewis Carroll, the author of *Alice in Wonderland*, to the girl who was his inspiration for Alice. Her full name appears in the poem which is to be found at the end of *Through the Looking-Glass*.

A boat, beneath a summer sky
Lingering onward dreamily
In an evening of July –

Children three that nestle near,
Eager eye and willing ear,
Pleased a simple tale to hear –

Long has paled that sunny sky:
Echoes fade and memories die:
Autumn frosts have slain July.

Still she haunts me, phantomwise,
Alice moving under skies
Never seen by waking eyes.

Children yet, the tale to hear,
Eager eye and willing ear,
Lovingly shall nestle near.

In a Wonderland they lie,
Dreaming as the days go by,
Dreaming as the summers die:

Ever drifting down the stream –
Lingering in the golden gleam –
Life, what is it but a dream?

17: Word games

Ghosts

A spelling game.

Aim of the game Players take it in turn to add letters to a word, but must avoid finishing it.

How you play

Any number can play. The players sit in a circle, and the play goes clockwise. The first player starts a word by saying a letter. The person to that player's left says another letter that will continue the word, but will not complete it. The third player adds another letter and so on. This continues until either someone finishes a word, or someone makes a challenge.

Making a challenge If you think that someone has added a letter without having thought of a word that can be made from it, you can challenge them. If they prove that the letter they have added will make a word, then you lose a life. If they cannot prove it, then they lose a life.

Scoring Everyone starts with three lives. If you finish a word, you lose a life. If you make a wrong challenge, you lose a life. If you are challenged correctly you lose a life. When you have lost all three lives, you are out. The last person still alive is the winner.

Player	What they say	Word they are thinking of
ANNA	M	
MARK	I	Mist
MARY	N	Mind
TOM	U	Minute
ANNA	T	Minute
MARK	E	
ANNA	That finishes a word, so Mark loses a life.	
MARY	My turn. Z	
TOM	O	Zoo
ANNA	N	Zone
MARK	A	Zonal
MARY	I challenge that.	
MARK	The word I was thinking of was 'zonal'.	
TOM	That's all right. Mary loses a life. My turn.	

Personal favourites

Aim of the game To find answers to different questions using only words beginning with your own initials.

How you play

Any number can play. One person asks the rest of the players a question. Each of them has to answer with two words that begin with the same letters as his or her first name and surname. For example, the question might be, 'What do you like doing in the holidays?' Peter Clarke could reply, 'Playing cricket', Mary Ransome could say, 'Making rissoles', and so on. When everyone has answered, another person asks a question.

Scoring Anyone who cannot answer correctly loses a point. At the end of the game, the person with the lowest number of penalty points is the winner.

165

First and last

A spelling game.

Aim of the game   To continue a list of words by thinking of a word that starts with the last letter of the previous word.

How you play

Any number can play. The players sit in a circle and play goes round clockwise. The players decide on a category: for example, animals, or towns, or girls' names. The first player says a word in that category. The second player then has to say another word in that category that begins with the last letter of the previous word.

For example, if the category was animals, the word chain might be: *horse ... elephant ... tiger ... rat ... etc.*

Each player only has five seconds to think of a word. If you cannot do that, or if you choose a word that begins with the wrong letter, or one that has already been chosen, then you are out.

Scoring   You win a round by being the last person left in. When you win a round, you score a point.

Going on a journey

Aim of the game   Answering questions using words that
                        begin with different letters of the
                        alphabet.

─── **How you play** ───

Any number can play. The first player starts with the letter 'A'.
She says, 'I am going to . . .' and finishes with the name of a
place beginning with 'A', for example, Athens. The player to
her left then asks her a question, for example, 'What are you
going to do there?' The first player has to answer using three
words that begin with A. For example, she might say, 'I'm going
to ask for ancient antiques.' Then the second player says, 'I am
going to . . .' and finishes with a place beginning with B. She, in
turn, is asked a question by the player on her left, and so on.

Scoring   Any player who cannot answer the
                question satisfactorily loses a point. The
                player with the highest score is the
                winner.

The word square game

This simple game is based on the principle of the word square. Players have a pencil and paper. They draw a grid of 6 × 6 or 7 × 7 squares:

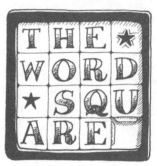

How you play

Each player takes it in turn to call out a letter. As each letter is called out, everyone must write it in one of the squares. The object is to make words across and down, as in a crossword. Individual letters can be used in both across and down words, but words going in the same direction must not join up. So, for example:

ABLE HIT
N
D

makes three words: able, hit, and

ABLEHIT
N
D

only makes one word: and

Players are not allowed to move letters or rub them out, once they have been written in. The game ends when all the squares have been filled in. Players then score the words they have made:

2 letter word 2 points
3   3
4   4
5   6
6   8
7   10

The player with the highest score is the winner.

Taboo

A game for quick thinkers and expert spellers.

Aim of the game   To avoid using words containing a certain letter.

How you play

Any number can play. One player is chosen as questioner. A letter is chosen. The questioner asks each of the others in turn a different question. In their answers they must avoid using the chosen letter. They must answer without hesitating and their answers must make sense.

Scoring   Anyone who uses the forbidden letter, or hesitates, or gives an answer that doesn't make sense, or doesn't answer at all, is out. The last person left in wins the round and is the questioner for the next round.

The acrostics game

You can turn acrostics into a word game.
There are two versions: a simple one and
a more difficult one.

Version 1

A word of 6–8 letters is chosen. Each player writes it down the
left-hand side of his paper. For example:

GREATLY

Then a category is chosen, for example, animals. Each player
has to think of names of animals that begin with each of the
letters. For example:

Giraffe	Tiger
Rhinoceros	Leopard
Eland	Yak
Antelope	

The first person to finish wins that round. You then go on to
another category, keeping the same word. When you have
exhausted the possibilities of that word, you choose another,
and so on.

Version 2

In version 2, you begin in the same way, but it is better to choose a slightly longer word. For example:

DISPLEASURE

Players then have to make up one word beginning with each of those letters. The snag is that you may only use the letters of the original word, and you can only use them as many times as they occur in the original word. Also you are not allowed to use words that form shorter parts of the original word. (In this case, for example, 'pleasure' would not be allowed, but 'please' would.) When you have all finished, you add up the total number of letters. The player with the highest score is the winner. Here is one answer for 'displeasure':

> DISPLEASE (9)
> IDLERS (6)
> SPIRES (6)
> PLEASED (7)
> LEISURE (7)
> EASED (5)
> ASSURED (7)
> SPIDERS (7)
> USED (4)
> REISSUED (8)
> EASIER (6)

Total score: 72

Answers

Page 154: man
Page 155: an egg, time
Page 157: illegal, tulips, rocket, ragtime, tears
Page 158: you're under arrest, six of one and half a dozen of the other, spinach, I understand
Page 161: conversation, nuclear, point, punishment, semolina, train, Clint Eastwood, Margaret Thatcher, Mary Whitehouse, William Shakespeare

INDEX

Oxford University Press, Walton Street, Oxford OX2 6DP

Oxford New York Toronto
Delhi Bombay Calcutta Madras Karachi
Petaling Jaya Singapore Hong Kong Tokyo
Nairobi Dar es Salaam Cape Town
Melbourne Auckland

and associated companies in
Berlin Ibadan

Oxford is a trade mark of Oxford University Press

© Elizabeth and John Seely 1990

0 19 831167 2

Set by Tradespools Ltd, Frome, Somerset

Printed in Great Britain at the
University Press, Cambridge

Acknowledgements

The illustrations are by Debbie Clark, Jan Lewis,
Shoo Rayner amd Axel Scheffler.

*The publishers would like to thank the following for
permission to reproduce the photographs:*

Apple Computer UK, p.23 (bottom); BBC Enterprises
p.32 (top); the Dandy/D.C. Thompson & Co Ltd p.20,
118; Mary Evans Picture Library p.23 (middle), 55;
Format Partners - Photo Library p. 7 (middle left,
bottom right); Keith Gibson p.18 (bottom left); Hamish
Hamilton p.18 (bottom left); The Hutchison Library
p.35 (right); Rob Judges p.7 (top left and right); The
Mansell collection p.163; Military Archive and
Research Services p.7 (middle right); Spectrum Colour
Library p.7 (bottom left), p.35 (left).

*We are grateful to the following for permission to
reprint copyright material:*

Vivien Alcock: from *Shades of Dark,* (Lutterworth
Press), by permission of the publishers. Alan Ayck-
bourn: from *Ernie's Incredible Illucinations,* (Hutchin-
son Education), by permission of the author. Kit
Wright: from *Poems for over-0-year-olds,* (Puffin
Books), by permission of the publisher.